cook's essentials™

step-by-step cookbook

cook's essentials™
step-by-step cookbook

BOB WARDEN & MEREDITH LAURENCE
with the best of
CREATIVE COOK'S KITCHEN®

QVC PUBLISHING, INC.

QVC PUBLISHING, INC.

Jill Cohen, Vice President and Publisher
Ellen Bruzelius, General Manager
Karen Murgolo, Director of Acquisitions and Rights
Cassandra Reynolds, Publishing Assistant

Produced in association with International Masters Publishers, Inc.
Design by Susan DeAcutis, Senior Designer; Lucille Friedman, Managing Editor
Original Design by Amy Keith, Art Director; Lynn Naliboff, Project Editor

Q Publishing and colophon are trademarks of QVC Publishing, Inc.
cook's essentials™ is a trademark of QVC, Inc.
Copyright © 2002 International Masters Publishers AB.
Creative Cook's Kitchen® is a registered trademark of IMP AB.

Published by QVC Publishing, Inc., 50 Main Street, Mt. Kisco, New York 10549

Manufactured in the United States of America

ISBN: 1-928998-09-7

First Edition

10 9 8 7 6 5 4 3 2 1

contents

introduction

Congratulations on your purchase of the *cook's essentials™ step-by-step cookbook*. This book, like cook's essentials™ cookware and bakeware, was created at your request. Thanks to your suggestions, ideas and loyalty, over eight million pieces of cook's essentials™ cookware are being used in kitchens across the country. Our customers have helped make cook's essentials stainless steel products the best-selling brand of stainless nonstick cookware in America! Cook's essentials™ hard-coat-enamel and hard-anodized lines are widely recognized as the finest value for their cost in the world. We have enjoyed tremendous success with our cook's essentials™ bakeware as well; it is only a year old and already has over one million pieces in use.

We have listened to your requests for a cookbook, and we expect this one to exceed your expectations. We searched the country for great recipes and we found them with the experts at Creative Cook's Kitchen®. These recipes were developed and tested to provide the home cook with classic dishes and more—all with a creative flair that is sure to please family and friends. In fact, Creative Cook's Kitchen® has developed thousands of recipes over the years, so we chose the hundred or so recipes and variations we thought would be the best to use with cooks essentials™ products. And since we're assuming that everyone would like a little help in the kitchen, each recipe is written with easy-to-follow directions and illustrated with six beautiful color photographs—over 500 photos all together! So anyone can pick up a cook's essentials™ skillet or cookie sheet and make an impressive meal or dessert that their family will enjoy. Although the recipes in this book are selected with cook's essentials™ products in mind, they can be used successfully with other quality cookware and bakeware.

We have selected recipes that give you a broad range of cooking and baking options. A dozen tasty hors d'oeuvres recipes begin the book, followed by recipes for skillet meals, great roasts, and our favorite one-dish meals. Simple side dishes with a dozen easy new twists help complete any meal. We have also included three-dozen great bread, cookie, cake and pie recipes.

We believe this colorful, step-by-step cookbook produced with the Creative Cook's Kitchen® expertise will help you become even more creative and successful using your cook's essentials™ cookware and bakeware. We will continue to introduce new and innovative products at your request, and plan to publish more product-specific cookbooks in the future. To make it easier for you to send us your requests, we have created a special link to our QVC cook's essentials™ website for your suggestions. Let us know what you want, and you can help make our next cook's essentials™ cookbook even better. Have fun with this book, and give us a call from time to time to tell us how you're cooking.

Enjoy!

Bob Warden and Meredith Laurence

cook's essentials™ Stainless Steel cookware combines metal-utensil-safe DuPont Non-Stick Coating with a durable stainless steel alloy and a heavy gauge aluminum-impact bonded base—an excellent and even heat conductor.

Designed so heat travels up all sides of the pan, hard-anodized aluminum provides efficient cooking with less heat. Twice as hard as steel, anodized aluminum is almost impossible to nick or scratch.

Available in several high gloss colors, porcelain enamel exteriors are baked at high temperatures to create a tough, long lasting luster. These pots and pans have a tempered glass, dome-style lid and stay-cool riveted handles that won't need to be tightened.

The cook's essentials™ line of bakeware is specially treated to resist rust and corrosion. Made of tin-free steel, these pans provide perfect heat conductivity for even, thorough baking. And, with DuPont's Non-Stick Coating with ScratchGuard™, your baked goods will pop right out of the pans.

Whether you're cooking a festive meal for a crowd or just a quick weekday meal for yourself and your family, you'll be able to find many great ideas in this new cookbook. With the expert, easy, step-by-step recipes from Creative Cook's Kitchen® and the professional quality of cook's essentials™ cookware, you'll leave the kitchen feeling like you're a pro!

hors d'oeuvres—This chapter offers fun ideas for parties or tasty snacks. From a hearty Antipasto Platter to exotic Coconut-Fried Shrimp, you'll be able to please everyone in your crowd. Included here are classic favorites such as Savory Devilled Eggs and Stuffed Mushroom Caps.

skillet meals—Delicious recipes like Chicken Cordon Bleu, Cajun Blackened Catfish and Cranberry Pork Chops are all made here in a simple skillet. Start with a nonstick skillet and the right ingredients and in a few easy steps you can have a main dish worthy of a great restaurant!

roasting—Whether you'd like to feed a crowd with a Perfect Prime Rib or just have a comforting Sunday family dinner of roast chicken, you'll find dozens of ideas for easy, wholesome roasts that you simply prepare and pop in the oven. Using a cook's essentials™ roaster makes for foolproof cooking and timesaving clean-up.

one-dish meals—What could be more appealing than having a complete meal ready after cooking only one recipe? Choose from Mexican Casserole, Veggie and Pasta Oven Omelet and lots more. The terrific recipes in this chapter use everything from cook's essentials™ skillets to stock pots to baking sheets, and most cookware goes from stovetop to oven, making preparation even easier.

side dishes—For those recipes that aren't a complete meal, you'll want to prepare a side dish of a tasty and nutritious vegetable or a refreshing, crisp salad. From colorful Coleslaw to Cashew Broccoli au Gratin, any meal can be rounded out in style.

breads—As the Italians say, "A meal is not complete without bread." This chapter shows you dozens of wonderful ways to complete your meal: from Garlic Sage Knots to Savory Pesto Swirls. Or for those with a sweet tooth, try Banana-Pecan Bread or Magic Cookie-Dough Muffins. Even beginning cooks will get the step-by-step help they need from Creative Cook's Kitchen® to make breadmaking fun and easy.

cookies—The smell of freshly-baked cookies brings out the kid in all of us. Use a cooks essentials™ cookie sheet or cookie pan to make treats that make your mouth water—from the winsome Cow Spot Cookies to the chock-full-of-sweetness White Chocolate Blondies. In fact, you might consider doubling the recipe so you have enough cookies to go around!

cakes and pies—For those special occasions—or just for a treat—you'll want to know how to whip up a cake or pie that is truly special. From Summer Strawberry Pie to Decadent Chocolate Cake—there's a scrumptious recipe for every taste and occasion.

Antipasto Platter

CUTTING THE VEGETABLES

1. Cut potatoes into 1-inch chunks. Cut each onion into 6 wedges. Cut tops off bell peppers; remove cores. Using a spoon, scrape out seeds; discard. Cut peppers into 1-inch strips. ▼

ROASTING THE VEGETABLES

1. Preheat oven to 450°F. In a large shallow roasting pan, toss potatoes with olive oil, rosemary and salt. Bake potatoes for 10 minutes. Add bell peppers, onions and mushrooms to pan; toss to coat. Bake, stirring frequently, until vegetables are golden brown and tender, 20-25 minutes longer. Remove from oven.

DRESSING THE VEGETABLES

1. In a small bowl, combine vinegar, basil, mustard, garlic, salt and pepper; whisk until smooth. Pour dressing over roasted vegetables in pan; stir gently to coat. Let cool to room temperature. ▼

ARRANGING THE PLATTER

1. Stack wedges of bread, points upward, in the center of a serving platter. ▼

2. Separate potatoes, onions and peppers; arrange in piles on the platter. Place prosciutto, cherry tomatoes, cheese, anchovies, olives and artichoke hearts in piles around the bread.

Attention to Detail

You can add anything to an antipasto platter. Personalize yours with your favorite ingredients—any of these would be delicious!

- oil-packed tuna • sardines • anchovies • dry-cured Italian sausage
- hard-cooked, deviled or stuffed eggs • crumbled Gorgonzola
- radishes • carrot or celery sticks • capers

Appetizing Facts

Antipasto is Italian for "before the meal"; the term refers to an appetizer platter of raw, cooked or cured vegetables, meats, fish and cheeses. Pieces of hearty grilled or toasted bread, such as focaccia, are often included. The foods are in bite-size pieces and are easy to serve and eat.

Oil and Vinegar

Serve your antipasto platter with cruets of olive oil and balsamic or red-wine vinegar. Your guests can dress their favorite items from the platter as they desire.

GOOD IDEA For easy individual servings, thread the vegetables, meats and cheese on skewers; arrange around the pita triangles.

Variations

High Impact

Create a dramatic look for your antipasto platter by contrasting colors, shapes and textures. Try arranging items in stripes on a rectangular platter.

Seasoned Pita Wedges

Add zip to the platter with zesty pita wedges. Brush pitas with oil; sprinkle with Italian seasonings and red pepper flakes. Bake 5 minutes; cut into triangles.

Bacon-Wrapped Scallops

You Will Need

FOR THE TOPPING
- 1 cup bread crumbs
- 2 tablespoons butter, melted
- 1/4 cup diced red bell pepper
- 2 teaspoons chopped fresh parsley

FOR THE MARINADE
- 1/4 cup fresh lemon juice
- 1/4 cup olive oil
- 1/8 teaspoon salt
- 1/8 teaspoon freshly ground black pepper

FOR THE SCALLOPS
- 16 large sea scallops
- 8 slices bacon

SPECIAL AIDS
16 toothpicks

MAKES 16

**COOKING TIME
8 MINUTES**

MAKING THE TOPPING

1. In a small bowl, combine bread crumbs and butter. In a small skillet, heat bread crumb mixture over medium heat, stirring, until toasted and golden. Add diced red bell pepper.

PREPARING THE SCALLOPS

1. Rinse scallops under cold running water; pat dry with paper towels. Pull off the small white muscle. ▼

2. For the marinade, in a large bowl, combine lemon juice, oil, salt and pepper. Mix well. Add scallops, tossing to coat. Chill, covered, for 1 hour.

3. Preheat broiler. Line broiler pan with foil. Wrap each scallop with a slice of bacon. ▼

4. Secure bacon on scallop by placing a toothpick through the center. Place scallops on broiler pan. Broil, turning once, until scallops are tender and turn opaque, and bacon is cooked through, about 8 minutes. ▼

5. Sprinkle baked scallops evenly with crumb mixture; top with parsley. Serve immediately.

Attention to Detail

Seafood appetizers are traditionally served with cocktail sauce. A spicy combination of ketchup, horseradish and sometimes hot sauce, cocktail sauce enhances any seafood snack.

COCKTAIL SAUCE

- 1/4 cup ketchup or chili sauce
- 1 tablespoon prepared horseradish
- 1/4 teaspoon Worcestershire sauce or hot pepper sauce
- 1 clove garlic, minced (optional)

In a small bowl, combine all ingredients. Cover bowl with plastic wrap; chill for 2 hours before serving.

Easy Switch
Instead of bacon, wrap scallops with long strips of ham or prosciutto for an easy substitute.

Serving Ideas
For a different presentation, serve these scallops on a platter with grilled shrimp and fresh fruit cubes on skewers.

Mini Bites
Small bay scallops can be used in place of the sea scallops. However, because they are so small, you may want to wrap two bay scallops with each piece of bacon.

GOOD IDEA This hearty appetizer is all you need for the start of a meal. Serve with crusty bread in place of a salad.

Variations

Shrimp Delights
Use shrimp instead of scallops. Simply substitute 1 pound medium shrimp, shelled and deveined.

Dipping Sauce
A honey mustard dipping sauce is a perfect complement to the scallops. Top sauce with some parsley before serving.

Brie in Puff Pastry

You Will Need

❧❧❧❧

FOR THE BRIE IN PUFF PASTRY

- 1   sheet frozen puff pastry (half of a 17¼-ounce package)
- 1   egg
- 1   tablespoon water
- 2   tablespoons butter or margarine
- ¼   pound mushrooms, chopped (about 1½ cups)
- 1   small onion, chopped (about ½ cup)
- 1   teaspoon sugar
- ½   teaspoon salt
- ¼   teaspoon freshly ground black pepper
- 1   wheel Brie cheese (about 16 ounces, approximately 6 inches in diameter)

FOR SERVING

assorted crackers and fresh fruit

SERVES 12

BAKING TIME 30 MINUTES

Kitchen Tips

- Freeze the unused sheet of puff pastry for a later use.
- For best results, use cold, firm Brie straight from the refrigerator. Work quickly to keep the cheese and pastry from getting too warm and soft before baking.
- The soft white rind on Brie is edible; don't try to remove it!

MAKING THE BRIE IN PUFF PASTRY

1. Thaw puff pastry sheet at room temperature for 30 minutes. Lightly grease a baking sheet.

2. Preheat oven to 400°F. In a small bowl, whisk egg and water; set aside.

3. In a medium skillet, melt butter over medium-high heat. Add chopped mushrooms and onion; sauté until softened, about 8 minutes.

4. Add sugar, salt and pepper to skillet; cook until onion and mushrooms are golden, about 3 minutes. Remove from heat; cool completely.

5. Unfold puff pastry on a lightly floured surface. Using a lightly floured rolling pin, roll pastry into a 14-inch square. Trim the pastry to make a round about 12 inches in diameter.

6. Spoon the onion and mushroom mixture into the center of the pastry round; spread to approximate diameter of Brie wheel. Top with Brie. ▼

7. Brush edges of round with egg wash. Fold pastry edges over Brie. Press pastry edges together firmly to seal. ▼

8. Place the wrapped Brie seam-side down on prepared baking sheet. Make decorations for top using pastry scraps: For grapes, roll small pieces of pastry (about ¼-inch square) into balls. For vines, use a sharp knife to make ropes 4-8 inches long and ¼ inch wide. Place grapes in 3 clusters on top of pastry. Twist vines across top to connect grape clusters. Brush pastry with egg wash. ▼

9. Bake until pastry is golden, about 20 minutes. Let stand 1 hour. Serve with crackers and fruit.

Buying Brie

Brie is produced in several countries, including the United States, but French Brie is considered the best. Select Brie that is plump and springy to the touch.

Cheese Choice

Camembert, another soft-ripened cheese, is a good alternative to Brie, but it has a slightly stronger flavor.

Make Ahead

You can make baked Brie up to 2 days ahead. Refrigerate in an airtight container. Just before serving, reheat at 350°F for 15-20 minutes.

■ GOOD IDEA

Hosting an elegant reception at home? Serve this baked Brie with crackers, fruit and wine.

Variations

Easy Elegance

Fruit and Brie make a beautiful pair. Warm plain Brie at 350°F until soft, 15-20 minutes. Serve with assorted fresh fruit.

Cheese Puffs

For cocktail party appetizers, cut puff pastry into squares and top with pieces of Brie. Fold pastry corners over the cheese and twist. Bake at 425°F for 12-15 minutes.

Broccoli-Cheese Nuggets

You Will Need

❦❦❦❦❦

FOR THE BROCCOLI-CHEESE NUGGETS

- 1 package (16 ounces) frozen broccoli florets, thawed
- 2 cups shredded extra-sharp Cheddar cheese
- 2/3 cup dehydrated potato flakes
- 1/4 cup grated Parmesan cheese
- 4 slices cooked ham, diced (about 1 cup)
- 2 large eggs
- 1 teaspoon Dijon-style mustard
- 1 teaspoon salt
- 1/4 teaspoon freshly ground black pepper

SERVES 6

**BAKING TIME
20 MINUTES**

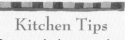

Kitchen Tips

- Do not substitute powdered potato for potato flakes; it will affect the taste and texture of the nuggets.

- It is important to let the mixture stand before baking so the potato flakes can absorb moisture.

MAKING THE NUGGETS

1. Cook broccoli according to package directions. Drain cooked broccoli thoroughly in a colander, pressing with the back of a wooden spoon to remove excess water. Chop broccoli into 1/4-inch pieces. ▼

2. Preheat oven to 400°F. Generously grease a large baking sheet.

3. In a large bowl, combine broccoli, Cheddar, potato flakes, Parmesan, ham, eggs, mustard, salt and pepper; stir until mixture is thoroughly blended. Let stand for about 10 minutes.

4. Drop generous tablespoonfuls of mixture, about 1 inch apart, onto the prepared baking sheet. ▼

5. Bake nuggets until golden brown around the edges, about 20 minutes. Using a spatula, remove nuggets from baking sheet and transfer to platter; serve immediately.

Attention to Detail

Turn this savory snack into a satisfying meal—just follow this recipe:

TASTY TUNA NUGGETS

- 1 can (9 ounces) tuna in water, drained
- 1 package (10 ounces) frozen chopped spinach, thawed and drained
- 3/4 cup bread crumbs
- 1/2 cup shredded Monterey Jack cheese
- 1/4 cup Parmesan cheese
- 2 eggs
- 1 teaspoon minced onion
- 1 teaspoon salt

1. Preheat oven to 375°F. Spray a baking sheet with vegetable cooking spray.

2. In a large bowl, combine tuna, spinach, bread crumbs, Monterey Jack, Parmesan, eggs, onion and salt; mix well.

3. Drop generous tablespoonfuls of mixture, about 1 inch apart, onto the prepared baking sheet.

4. Bake 15 minutes; turn nuggets over and bake 10 minutes longer. Serve immediately.

Popeye Special

Dislike broccoli? Don't be discouraged—just substitute frozen chopped spinach and use mozzarella cheese instead of Cheddar.

Go Veggie

For a meatless main dish, omit the ham and shape the cheese mixture into 3-inch patties. Coat patties with egg and crumbs, then deep-fry. Serve with warm marinara or lemon sauce.

Broccoli Brunch

Fill omelettes with this tasty broccoli-cheese mixture, then sprinkle extra cheese on top before serving.

GOOD IDEA Serve these cheesy morsels as part of an appetizer buffet with some peppers, olives, tomatoes and pepperoni.

Variations

Patty-Cakes

You can form this broccoli-cheese mixture into patty shapes, too. Serve them as a side dish, or as a light lunch with a green salad or on a sesame-seed bun.

Gad-Zukes

These nuggets are also tasty with blanched, diced zucchini instead of the broccoli. Fresh or dried oregano adds interest to this mild-flavored vegetable.

Coconut Shrimp

You Will Need

❦❦❦❦

FOR THE DIPPING SAUCE

- ¼ cup freshly squeezed lime juice
- ¼ cup soy sauce
- 2 tablespoons honey
- 1 teaspoon grated lime zest

FOR THE SHRIMP

- ½ cup coconut milk (from a 15-ounce can)
- ¼ cup all-purpose flour
- 1 large egg
- 1½ teaspoons curry powder
- 1½ cups unsweetened shredded coconut
- 1 pound large shrimp, peeled and deveined, with tails (18-20 shrimp)
- vegetable oil for frying
- 1 teaspoon salt
- ⅛ teaspoon cayenne pepper
- 1 lime, cut into wedges

SPECIAL AIDS

deep-fat thermometer

SERVES 4

**COOKING TIME
4 MINUTES PER BATCH**

Kitchen Tips

If you can't find unsweetened coconut, pour boiling water over some sweetened coconut and let stand for 5 minutes. Drain, rinse and dry coconut with paper towels; place on a plate and let stand overnight.

MAKING THE DIPPING SAUCE

1. In a small bowl, combine lime juice, soy sauce, honey and lime zest, stirring until blended and smooth; set aside.

MAKING THE SHRIMP

1. In a medium bowl, whisk coconut milk, flour, egg and curry powder until blended and smooth. ▼

2. Set a wire rack over a baking sheet. Line another baking sheet with waxed paper; spread coconut on the paper.

3. Working with 1 shrimp at a time and holding it firmly by the tail, dip shrimp into batter, shaking off excess. Dredge shrimp in coconut and transfer to the prepared rack. Continue coating remaining shrimp. ▼

---

4. Line a plate with paper towels. In a deep heavy skillet, heat about 3 inches of vegetable oil over medium-high heat until it registers 350°F on a deep-fat thermometer.

5. Add shrimp to the skillet, about six at a time. Cook, turning once, until golden, about 4 minutes. Transfer shrimp to the prepared plate. Continue cooking remaining shrimp in batches. ▼

SERVING THE SHRIMP

1. Transfer shrimp to a serving platter. In a small bowl, mix salt and cayenne; sprinkle over shrimp. Serve with reserved dipping sauce and lime wedges.

Attention to Detail

Make a cool cup for the dipping sauce:

CUCUMBER CUP

Cut a cucumber crosswise into a 2½-inch-long piece. Using a small sharp-edged teaspoon or a melon baller, scoop out a well in the center of the cucumber piece to within ½ inch of the edges. Pour dipping sauce into the cup and serve with the coconut-fried shrimp.

Hot Stuff

If you like appetizers on the spicy side, just double the amount of cayenne pepper and curry powder in this tasty recipe.

Theme Snack

For a fun presentation, serve these shrimp with tropical-motif cocktail napkins and festive toothpicks.

Tropical Taste

Here's another great combination that uses coconut flavor: For a salad, combine cubes of cooked chicken, soy sauce, coconut milk, pineapple and orange wedges; serve it in a pineapple shell.

■ GOOD IDEA Bright tropical fruit is the perfect garnish for this dish: Try star fruit, mango, kiwifruit or lime wedges.

Variations

Main-Course Shrimp
These snacking shrimp become a delicious dinner when served with steamed rice and snow peas.

Coconut-Fried Chicken
Use the same batter and coconut coating for strips of chicken breast and serve with a tropical fruit salsa.

Crispy Vegetable Pockets

You Will Need

✿✿✿✿

FOR THE DIPPING SAUCE

- ½ cup peach or apricot preserves
- 1 tablespoon plus 1 teaspoon cider vinegar
- 2 teaspoons soy sauce
- 2 teaspoons sesame oil

FOR THE VEGETABLE POCKETS

- 1 tablespoon vegetable oil
- 1 tablespoon sesame oil
- 1 tablespoon coarsely grated fresh gingerroot
- 3 green onions, chopped (about ⅓ cup)
- 2 medium cloves garlic, minced (about 1 teaspoon)
- 2 cups grated cabbage
- 7 shiitake or white mushrooms, caps only, finely chopped
- 1 large carrot, grated (about ½ cup)
- 1 tablespoon soy sauce
- 32 wonton wrappers

SERVES 8

BAKING TIME 8 MINUTES

Kitchen Tips

- Wonton wrappers (or skins) can be round or square. Look for square ones to make these triangular pockets.
- You can make this filling 1-2 days in advance; bring to room temperature before filling wontons.

MAKING THE SAUCE

1. In a medium bowl, combine peach preserves, cider vinegar, soy sauce and sesame oil. Whisk until well blended.

MAKING THE FILLING

1. In a wok or large skillet, combine vegetable oil, sesame oil, gingerroot, green onions and garlic over medium-high heat; cook, stirring frequently, until mixture becomes fragrant, about 2 minutes.

2. Add cabbage, mushrooms and carrot; continue stirring over medium heat until mushrooms wilt and cabbage becomes slightly soft, about 3 minutes.

3. Add soy sauce; cook, stirring, until liquid is almost evaporated, about 2 minutes. Remove from heat; let cool.

MAKING THE VEGETABLE POCKETS

1. Preheat oven to 375°F. Grease 2 baking sheets. Fill a small bowl with water. Lay 10 wonton wrappers on a prepared baking sheet. Using your fingers, moisten wrapper edges lightly with water. ▼

2. Spoon about 1 tablespoon of filling along 1 corner of each wonton wrapper. Fold over the opposite corner, forming a triangle; press along both edges to seal well. ▼

3. Repeat with the remaining filling and wrappers.

BAKING THE VEGETABLE POCKETS

1. Working in batches, bake vegetable pockets until the bottoms are slightly browned, about 4 minutes. Using a spatula, turn over the pockets; continue to bake until the bottoms are slightly browned, about 4 minutes longer. ▼

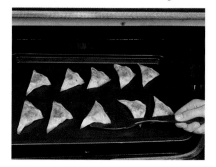

2. Serve vegetable pockets immediately with the dipping sauce.

Perfect Pockets

Make these vegetable pockets as a healthful, tasty alternative to egg rolls. They're made from smaller wonton wrappers, filled with fresh, colorful veggies and they're baked instead of fried—they make an ideal party hors d'oeuvre.

It's a Wrap!

Wonton wrappers can be found in the dairy or produce section of the grocery store.

Simple Garnish

Toast a handful of sesame seeds to sprinkle over the pockets for an easy and delicious garnish.

■ GOOD IDEA

Serve these pockets, along with spare ribs and green onion pancakes, for an all-Asian appetizer buffet!

Variations

Sweetly Wrapped

For an easy dessert, fill wonton wrappers with a mixture of raisins, cranberries and confectioners' sugar. Fry, then drizzle with an orange juice glaze.

Classic Egg Rolls

Make a traditional egg roll by adding ground pork to the stir-fry; roll up tightly, burrito-style, in egg roll wrappers and bake or deep-fry.

Roasted Garlic Bruschetta

You Will Need

❧❧❧❧❧

FOR THE BRUSCHETTA

1	loaf (16 ounces) French bread
4	tablespoons olive oil, divided
1	small onion, finely chopped (about ¼ cup)
6	plum tomatoes, seeded and chopped (about 2 cups)
¼	cup chopped pitted black olives
5	tablespoons chopped fresh basil, divided
1	tablespoon roasted garlic
½	teaspoon salt
¼	teaspoon black pepper
¼	cup freshly grated Parmesan or Romano cheese

SPECIAL AIDS
pastry brush

MAKES 24 BRUSCHETTA

PREPARATION TIME
20 MINUTES

Kitchen Tips

- When broiling the bread, leave the oven door slightly ajar so you can see when the bread is done.

- To roast a head of garlic, cut off the top third and drizzle with olive oil; wrap in foil and roast at 400°F until golden brown, about 1 hour.

PREPARING THE BREAD

1. Preheat broiler. Cut bread diagonally into 24 slices. ▼

2. Place the slices in a single layer on a large baking sheet. Place 2 tablespoons olive oil in a small bowl. Using a pastry brush, brush olive oil onto both sides of each slice of bread. ▼

3. Broil bread slices 4-5 inches from heat until they are lightly toasted, about 1 minute on each side. Set aside.

MAKING THE BRUSCHETTA

1. In a small skillet, heat remaining olive oil over medium heat. Add onion; sauté until just softened, about 5 minutes. Add tomatoes, olives, 3 tablespoons basil, roasted garlic, salt and pepper. Cook, stirring, until heated through, about 1 minute; remove from heat. Top each slice of bread with 2 tablespoons tomato mixture. Sprinkle each slice with grated Parmesan. ▼

2. Return bruschetta to the broiler. Broil until the cheese begins to melt, about 2 minutes.

3. Garnish bruschetta with remaining chopped basil. Serve immediately.

Attention to Detail

BRUSCHETTA TOPPINGS

Traditionally, bruschetta was simply thick slices of toasted bread, rubbed with garlic and olive oil. But you can top the bread with almost anything! Here are some ideas:

- Goat cheese, roasted red peppers and sage
- Sautéed mushrooms, diced eggplant and Parmesan
- Brie, roasted garlic and rosemary
- Yellow tomatoes, prosciutto and fresh basil

Name Game

The word *bruschetta* is derived from the Italian word *bruscare*, "to toast." Making bruschetta was part of an ancient Roman celebration of the first pressing of the olive oil in the fall.

Party Food

Once just a humble workman's lunch, bruschetta has now become the perfect party food. For casual or formal gatherings, top it with anything from cheese to meat to dried fruit—or any combination of these items. Use your own imagination to create special slices!

■ **GOOD IDEA** Prepare this simple bruschetta for your guests and offer a host of toppings so everyone can embellish their own.

Variations

Bruschetta Pizza

For a simpler version, use a prepared pizza crust; sprinkle with shredded mozzarella cheese, broil until bubbly and top with the tomato mixture.

Supper Slices

Turn bruschetta into a light summertime meal. Top the tomato mixture with thin strips of grilled chicken. Serve warm or at room temperature with a salad.

Sausage Turnovers

MAKING THE DOUGH

1. In a medium bowl, dissolve yeast and sugar in warm water. Let stand until it begins to foam, about 5-10 minutes.

2. Stir Parmesan, oil, salt and pepper into yeast mixture. Using an electric mixer set on low speed, beat in flour, ½ cup at a time, until soft dough forms.

3. On a floured surface, knead dough until smooth and elastic, 5-10 minutes, adding more flour to prevent sticking. Place dough in a large greased bowl, turning to coat. Cover loosely with a damp cloth; let rise in a warm place until doubled in size, about 40 minutes.

MAKING THE TURNOVERS

1. In a skillet, cook sausage over medium heat, stirring, until browned. Drain on paper towels. In a large bowl, combine sausage, bread crumbs, egg, Parmesan, parsley and thyme; mix well.

2. Grease 2 baking sheets. Punch down dough. On a floured surface, using a floured rolling pin, roll dough to ⅛-inch thickness. Using a knife, cut dough in squares and circles. ▼

3. Spoon filling into center of each dough piece. ▼

4. Brush edges with water. Fold dough to form packets. Place on baking sheets. Cover loosely; let rise 25 minutes. ▼

5. Preheat oven to 350°F. Brush turnovers with egg. Sprinkle with Parmesan. Bake about 12-15 minutes.

Attention to Detail

Make tart cups by pressing rounds of dough into mini muffin cups and baking until golden, about 12 minutes. Fill with sausage mixture.

Electric Mix

Instead of kneading by hand, use an electric mixer with a dough hook. Spray hook with vegetable cooking spray to prevent the dough from sticking.

Kneading Tip

Place a damp towel under the board on which you are kneading the dough to help keep the board in place.

Best Rising

Be sure there are no drafts where dough is rising. Drafts cause the dough to rise slowly and unevenly.

GOOD IDEA Serve the turnovers with a fresh tomato sauce drizzled over them, or place sauce in a bowl for dipping.

Variations

Sausage Pie

Roll the dough into 2 circles. Fit one into a pie plate; spoon sausage filling into crust. Top with remaining dough. Bake for 20 minutes.

Beggar's Purse

Pull the dough up around the filling and gather into a bunch at the top. Bake as directed. For a nice touch, tie bundles with chives.

Savory Devilled Eggs

You Will Need

FOR THE EGGS
12 large eggs

FOR THE TRADITIONAL FILLING
¼ cup mayonnaise

1 green onion, minced

1 tablespoon finely chopped dill pickle

1 teaspoon dry mustard powder

¼ teaspoon hot red pepper sauce (optional)

1 tablespoon paprika

FOR THE TOMATO-BASIL FILLING
¼ cup mayonnaise

1 green onion, minced

2 tablespoons finely chopped oil-packed sun-dried tomatoes

2 tablespoons finely chopped fresh basil, divided

SPECIAL AIDS
pastry bag fitted with a large star tip

SERVES 12

PREPARATION TIME 20 MINUTES

PREPARING THE EGGS

1. Place eggs in a single layer in a large saucepan. Add cold water, filling the pan to 1 inch above eggs. Cover pan; bring to a boil over high heat.

2. Remove pot from heat and let stand, covered, until the eggs are hard-boiled, about 15 minutes. Place eggs under cold running water. Peel eggs; cut in half. Using a spoon, remove yolks. ▼

MAKING THE TRADITIONAL FILLING

1. In a blender, combine 6 egg yolks, mayonnaise, green onion, chopped pickle, dry mustard and red pepper sauce; process until smooth, about 10 seconds. Spoon filling into a pastry bag fitted with a large star tip. ▼

2. Pipe filling evenly into 6 egg white halves. Garnish with paprika. ▼

MAKING THE TOMATO-BASIL FILLING

1. In a blender, combine remaining egg yolks, mayonnaise, green onion, sun-dried tomatoes and 1 tablespoon basil. Process until smooth, about 7 seconds.

2. Spoon the filling into a pastry bag fitted with a large star tip. Pipe filling evenly into remaining egg white halves. Garnish with remaining basil.

Attention to Detail

PERFECTLY BOILED EGGS

It's easy to make the perfect boiled egg. In fact, "hard-boiled" eggs aren't actually boiled! When the water begins to boil, the pan is removed from heat. As the eggs stand in the hot water, the cooking process is completed. (This also prevents the greenish-gray color that sometimes appears around the edges of the yolk.)

For easier peeling, crack the shells, cool slightly under running water and then plunge into ice-cold water. Let the eggs stand in the water until cold.

Devilish Foods

Although the word "deviled" is usually applied to eggs, it can describe any spicy dish that includes mustard or hot red pepper.

Quick Mash

For fast deviled eggs, mash the egg yolk mixture with a fork and spoon the filling into the egg whites.

Make Ahead

You can prepare the hard-boiled eggs and fillings a day ahead and store them in the refrigerator; stuff the egg whites right before you are ready to serve.

■ **GOOD IDEA** Present these appetizers on a bed of salad greens and garnish the platter with olives and fresh herbs.

Variations

Deviled Egg Sandwich
Convert these deviled egg recipes into hearty sandwich fillings! Just chop the whole eggs; then add the rest of the ingredients, increasing the mayonnaise to $1/3$ cup.

Spicy Salmon Eggs
For another filling flavor, combine the eggs with drained flaked salmon; add a bit of spicy brown mustard and Worcestershire sauce.

Spicy Cajun Snack Mix

You Will Need

FOR THE CAJUN SPICE MIX

- ½ cup (1 stick) butter or margarine
- 1 teaspoon paprika
- 1 teaspoon seasoned salt
- ¾ teaspoon ground cumin
- ¾ teaspoon garlic powder
- ½ teaspoon dried basil
- ½ teaspoon dried thyme
- ¼ teaspoon freshly ground black pepper
- ⅛ teaspoon ground cayenne pepper

FOR THE SNACK MIX

- 2 cups bite-size crispy corn square cereal
- 2 cups bite-size crispy wheat square cereal
- 2 cups bite-size crispy rice square cereal
- 1 can (12 ounces) dry-roasted peanuts
- 1 cup mini pretzels

MAKES 9 CUPS

BAKING TIME
40-45 MINUTES

Kitchen Tips

This snack mix can be made ahead for any special occasion and it will stay fresh for several weeks. Simply store it at room temperature in an airtight container.

MAKING THE CAJUN SPICE MIX

1. Preheat oven to 250°F. Place butter in a 13- x 9-inch baking pan. Melt butter in oven, about 3 minutes.

2. In a large bowl, combine paprika, seasoned salt, cumin, garlic powder, basil, thyme, black pepper and cayenne pepper.

3. Remove the pan from the oven. Add the Cajun spice mix into the melted butter; mix thoroughly. ▼

BAKING THE SNACK MIX

1. Pour cereals, peanuts and pretzels into the pan. Toss lightly to coat. ▼

2. Bake the mix, stirring occasionally, until heated through and slightly browned, 40-45 minutes. ▼

3. Transfer the pan to a wire rack; cool snack mix completely before serving.

Attention to Detail

For a quick party solution, use the seasonings from the snack mix to prepare these savory chicken wings.

CRISPY CAJUN CHICKEN WINGS

- 24 small chicken wings (about 4 pounds)
- ½ cup Cajun spice mix
- ⅓ cup butter or margarine, melted
- 3 tablespoons vinegar

1. Preheat oven to 400°F. Dredge chicken wings in Cajun spice mix.

2. Mix melted butter and vinegar. Dip dredged wings in mixture; transfer to ungreased baking sheet.

3. Bake 15-20 minutes. Increase oven heat to 450°F. Turn chicken wings; bake until browned, 20-25 minutes longer.

Versatile Mix

For an instant snack, toss this mix with just about any nuts, cereals and crackers you have on hand! Try cashews or almonds, unsweetened puffed cereals, mini bagel chips, oyster crackers or cheese-flavored fish crackers.

"Souper" Idea

For a burst of flavor in your next bowl of soup, sprinkle in this snack mix instead of crackers.

Lunch Munch

Spice up a brown bag lunch with this snack mix—just be sure to pack a beverage!

■ GOOD IDEA Mix up a big batch of this spicy, savory snack and serve it at a Superbowl party—it will really heat things up!

Variations

Gift Mix

For a zesty gift, make an extra-large batch of the seasoning mix and pack it in cellophane bags. Tie with ribbon and attach a card with recipe ideas.

Flavorful Bread

Give frozen bread dough a little kick: Combine seasoning mix with 2 tablespoons olive oil or melted butter; spread over rolls before baking.

Stuffed Mushroom Caps

You Will Need

FOR THE MUSHROOMS

24 medium white mushrooms, wiped clean

2 tablespoons vegetable oil

FOR THE FILLING

4 slices bacon, finely diced

1 large clove garlic, minced

1 package (10 ounces) frozen chopped spinach, thawed and patted dry

¼ cup grated Parmesan cheese

1-2 tablespoons bread crumbs

¼ teaspoon black pepper

SERVES 8

**COOKING TIME
20 MINUTES**

Kitchen Tips

• When buying mushrooms, select those that are firm and evenly colored with tightly closed caps.

• Mushrooms should never be soaked in water because they absorb liquid and will become mushy.

• To keep white mushrooms from discoloring, squeeze the juice of one quarter lemon onto paper towels and wipe each cap with the dampened towel. This also helps clean the mushrooms.

• For easy stem removal, simply twist stem away from cap or use the tip of a small, sharp knife to release it.

PREPARING THE MUSHROOMS

1. Preheat oven to 400°F. Lightly grease a baking sheet. Carefully remove mushroom stems from caps. Chop stems finely; set aside. ▼

2. Score caps using a small sharp knife. Hold caps upside down and run the knife part way through the flesh, slicing on an angle and turning the caps as you work. Brush lightly with vegetable oil. ▼

MAKING THE FILLING

1. In a large skillet, cook bacon over medium-high heat until crisp, about 4 minutes. Using a slotted spoon, transfer bacon to paper towels; drain.

2. Add chopped mushroom stems and garlic to pan drippings; cook, stirring until most of the moisture has evaporated, 3-4 minutes. Add spinach; stir until mixture is heated through, 2-3 minutes longer. Add reserved bacon, Parmesan, bread crumbs and pepper.

STUFFING THE MUSHROOMS

1. Spoon filling into mushroom caps. Place on prepared baking sheet. Bake mushrooms until cooked through, 10-12 minutes. ▼

Attention to Detail

• You can create a more elaborate design on the mushroom caps by actually removing small wedges of flesh instead of just scoring the mushrooms. Use a small sharp knife and hold the mushroom carefully to avoid cutting yourself.

• For an especially nice touch, cut the tops of mushroom caps in a spiral pattern and use them to garnish your serving platter.

What to Buy

White mushrooms (also called white buttons) of uniform size and grade are available in 8- to 24-ounce packages. Alternatively, you can select individual mushrooms from bulk bins in your grocer's produce department.

Flavor Boost

For a slightly more robust flavor, try using cremini mushrooms in this recipe. They look very similar to the white variety except they are slightly larger and have light brown caps.

■ **GOOD IDEA** When it's your turn to bring hors d'oeuvres, place caps on a bed of fresh baby spinach leaves for easy transport.

Variations

Vegetable Stuffers
Bake this tasty filling in large cherry tomatoes. Or try it in portobello mushrooms, halved eggplants or zucchini boats.

Instant Stuffing
Make it easy on yourself. Use prepared frozen spinach soufflé to stuff mushroom caps. Serve with lemon wedges if you like.

Vegetable Chips

You Will Need

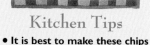

FOR THE CHIPS

- 1 large beet
- 1 large carrot
- 1 thick parsnip
- 1 sweet potato
- 1 Yukon gold potato

canola oil for frying

FOR THE SEASONING MIX

- 2 teaspoons kosher salt
- 1/4 teaspoon garlic powder
- 1/4 teaspoon onion powder

SPECIAL AIDS

mandoline

deep-fat thermometer

SERVES 6

COOKING TIME
15 MINUTES

Kitchen Tips

- It is best to make these chips on a dry sunny day, because wet weather and high humidity can make the chips soggy.
- The vegetables can be peeled and sliced up to 3 hours ahead; keep covered in cold water.
- Kosher salt is called for in this recipe because it adds flavor and texture.

PREPARING THE VEGETABLES

1. Peel vegetables; discard small end pieces of carrot and parsnip. Using a mandoline, a food processor fitted with a slicer attachment or a sharp knife, cut the vegetables into 1/16-inch slices. ▼

2. Fill a large bowl three-quarters full with ice water; transfer carrot, parsnip, sweet potato and Yukon gold to the bowl of water. Fill a small bowl three-quarters full with ice water; transfer beet slices to the bowl of water. Set aside both bowls for 30 minutes.

3. Line 2 baking sheets with several layers of paper towels. Drain vegetables and arrange in a single layer on the prepared baking sheets. Pat vegetables dry to remove excess moisture. ▼

FRYING THE VEGETABLES

1. Preheat oven to 200°F. Line 2 baking sheets or plates with paper towels. In a large saucepan, heat 3 inches canola oil over medium-high heat until it registers 375°F on a deep-fat thermometer, about 9 minutes. Add 1/2 cup vegetable slices and fry until crisp and golden brown, about 2 minutes. Drain vegetables thoroughly on prepared baking sheets.

2. Remove paper towels; spread fried vegetables in single layers on the baking sheets and place in the oven to keep warm. Continue frying process with remaining vegetable slices.

SEASONING THE CHIPS

1. In a small bowl, combine kosher salt, garlic powder and onion powder. Place warm vegetable chips in a large bowl; sprinkle mixture over chips. ▼

Attention to Detail

USING A MANDOLINE

A mandoline has adjustable blades for thin or thick slicing and for julienne and french-fry cutting. It helps cut firm vegetables uniformly and precisely.

Versatile Mix

You can choose the root vegetables you want for this recipe. Try beets, yams, white potatoes or rutabaga. Exotic veggies such as taro, with its purplish-white flesh, and yucca are also tasty. They are available in specialty produce stores and some supermarkets.

Sweet Treats

To satisfy your sweet tooth and a craving for crunch at the same time, prepare chips using apples, pears, plantains and sweet potatoes. Replace the seasoning mix with cinnamon sugar.

GOOD IDEA Crushed potato chips add crunch to coatings for fried foods. Use some in place of bread crumbs in a favorite recipe.

Variations

Chip Switch

Tired of crackers? Use these chips as a base for appetizers. Try them with a cream cheese spread, topped with green onions.

Veggie Croutons

For a change of taste from croutons, choose vegetable chips as garnishes to add flair to soups or salads.

Chicken Cordon Bleu

You Will Need

❦❦❦❦❦

FOR THE CHICKEN

- 4 boneless, skinless chicken breast halves (about 5 ounces each)
- 4 thin slices prosciutto or baked ham (about 1 ounce)
- 4 thin slices Gruyère or Swiss cheese (about 2 ounces)
- 8 large fresh basil leaves

FOR THE COATING

- ¾ cup plain bread crumbs
- 3 tablespoons finely chopped fresh parsley
- ½ teaspoon salt
- ½ teaspoon freshly ground black pepper
- 1 large egg
- 3 tablespoons olive oil

SPECIAL AIDS

kitchen mallet

SERVES 4

COOKING TIME 6-8 MINUTES

Kitchen Tips

- If you don't have a kitchen mallet, you can use the back side of a cleaver to pound the chicken breasts.
- For a nice touch, warm the serving plates in your oven for a few minutes just before serving the finished chicken.

FILLING THE CHICKEN

1. Place each chicken breast half between two sheets of waxed paper. Using a kitchen mallet, flatten until very thin, about ¼ inch thick.

2. Layer 1 slice prosciutto, 1 slice cheese and 2 basil leaves lengthwise over each breast half, leaving a ½-inch border; trim filling to fit, as needed. ▼

3. Fold ends of chicken in to cover filling, pressing the edges together to seal. Place seam side down on cutting board.

4. Using a large sharp knife, score the breast along the fold so the chicken will stay flat during cooking. ▼

COATING THE CHICKEN

1. Combine bread crumbs, parsley, salt and pepper in a pie plate or shallow dish.

2. In a small bowl, beat the egg. Dip the filled chicken breasts in egg, then dredge in crumb mixture. Set on waxed paper; let stand 10 minutes. ▼

COOKING THE CHICKEN

1. In a large nonstick skillet, heat oil over medium heat. Add chicken; cook 3-4 minutes on each side until browned.

Attention to Detail

After removing the cooked chicken breasts from the skillet, keep the pan warm and make a light sauce:

- Add chopped mushrooms and shallots as well as a little white wine to pan drippings in skillet.
- Heat until sauce is reduced and thickened.
- Place each breast on a dinner plate and spoon on sauce, or serve sauce in a gravy boat so dinner guests can add their own.

From Italy

Prosciutto is an Italian ham that has been seasoned, salt-cured, air-dried and pressed. *Prosciutto* is also the Italian word for "ham."

Did You Know?

Swiss cheese is actually a generic name for cheeses which have a slightly nutty flavor and a pale yellow flesh with large holes.

Grill It

For a summer feast, skip the coating and cook the stuffed chicken breasts on the grill. Sprinkle with grated cheese.

GOOD IDEA When guests drop by on short notice, Chicken Cordon Bleu makes a quick yet impressive meal.

Variations

Chicken Pinwheels

Make tasty and stunning hors d'oeuvres by slicing filled, cooked chicken crosswise. Garnish and serve.

On the Light Side

For a quick meal, place slices of chicken, ham and cheese on salad greens and drizzle with a warm vinaigrette.

Chicken Kiev

You Will Need

✿✿✿✿

FOR THE HERBED BUTTER

- **6** tablespoons (¾ stick) butter, softened
- **1** tablespoon chopped fresh parsley
- **1** teaspoon lemon juice
- **2** medium cloves garlic, minced
- **¼** teaspoon salt
- **¼** teaspoon black pepper
- **⅛** teaspoon cayenne pepper (optional)

FOR THE CHICKEN

- **4** large skinless, boneless chicken breast halves (about 1½ pounds)
- **½** cup all-purpose flour
- **¼** teaspoon salt
- **¼** teaspoon black pepper
- **1** egg
- **1** tablespoon water
- **¾** cup bread crumbs
- **2-3** cups vegetable oil

SPECIAL AIDS

waxed paper
kitchen mallet
deep-fat fryer or deep saucepan
deep-fat thermometer

SERVES 4

**COOKING TIME
12 MINUTES**

PREPARING THE HERBED BUTTER

1. In a small bowl, combine butter, parsley, lemon juice, garlic, salt, black pepper and cayenne pepper, if desired; mix well.

2. On a sheet of waxed paper, pat the mixture into a 3- x 1½-inch rectangle, about ½ inch thick. Freeze until firm, about 20 minutes.

3. Cut chilled butter lengthwise into 4 sticks; chill until ready to use. ▼

MAKING THE CHICKEN KIEV

1. Place a chicken breast half between 2 sheets of waxed paper; using the flat side of a kitchen mallet, pound the chicken firmly until it is about doubled in surface area and about ¼ inch thick.

2. Remove chicken from waxed paper and transfer to a clean work surface. Repeat with remaining chicken breasts.

3. Place 1 stick of herb butter along the short side of a chicken breast half. Starting at the short end, tightly roll the chicken up and over the butter. Continue to roll the chicken, folding the ends in and completely enclosing the butter. ▼

4. In a shallow dish, combine flour, salt and pepper. In another shallow dish, beat egg with water. Place bread crumbs in a third shallow dish. Dredge chicken rolls in seasoned flour mixture. Dip rolls in egg wash to coat; dredge in bread crumbs, patting so crumbs adhere. Cover chicken; chill at least 1 hour. ▼

5. Pour oil into a deep-fat fryer or deep saucepan to a 3-inch depth. Heat over medium-high heat until oil registers 375°F on a deep-fat thermometer. Add chicken in batches, being careful not to overcrowd; fry until dark brown, about 12 minutes. Serve immediately.

Butter Tip

This chicken dish is famed for its herbed-butter filling that spills out when the chicken is cut. If you allow the chicken to stand a few minutes before you cut it open, the chicken will absorb more of the flavorful butter.

Easy Switches

Replace the savory butter filling with other favorite flavors, such as herb Boursin cheese or drained cooked spinach. Or, try Cheddar cheese and chopped dried apricots for a taste combination that's sure to please!

■ **GOOD IDEA** To take full advantage of the herbed-butter filling, serve chicken Kiev on a bed of egg noodles or other pasta.

Variations

Seasoned Vegetables

This delicious side dish is a perfect accompaniment for the chicken Kiev: Sauté broccoli and cauliflower in a little of the herbed butter.

Herbed Butter

Form an extra batch of the flavorful butter into a cylinder; wrap in waxed paper and chill. Roll in paprika or chopped herbs. Serve with bread.

Easy Chicken Scaloppine

You Will Need

FOR THE VEGETABLES

- 1 tablespoon olive oil
- ½ red onion, thinly sliced (about 1 cup)
- 10 ounces white mushrooms, sliced (about 3 cups)
- 2 medium cloves garlic, minced (about 1 teaspoon)

FOR THE CHICKEN AND PASTA

- 4 large boneless, skinless chicken breast halves (about 1½ pounds total)
- ½ cup all-purpose flour
- 1 teaspoon dried sage
- ¼ teaspoon salt
- ¼ teaspoon black pepper
- 1-2 tablespoons olive oil
- 1-2 tablespoons butter or margarine
- ¼ cup balsamic vinegar or chicken broth
- 8 ounces angel hair pasta, cooked

fresh basil leaves

lemon wedges

SERVES 4

**COOKING TIME
22 MINUTES**

PREPARING THE VEGETABLES

1. In a large skillet, heat olive oil over medium-high heat. Add onion; sauté until softened, about 2 minutes. Add mushrooms and garlic; cook, stirring frequently, until vegetables are softened and lightly browned, 10-15 minutes. Cover and remove from heat; set aside.

MAKING THE CHICKEN AND PASTA

1. Rinse chicken breast halves under cold water; pat dry with paper towels. On a cutting board, cut each piece in half. Place between sheets of waxed paper; using a rolling pin, pound and roll chicken to a ¼-inch thickness. ▼

2. In a bowl, combine flour, sage, salt and pepper. Dredge chicken pieces in the mixture, shaking off excess. ▼

3. In a large skillet, heat 1 tablespoon olive oil and 1 tablespoon butter over medium heat. Cook chicken pieces, 4 or 5 at a time, until cooked through and lightly browned on both sides, about 2 minutes per side; add additional oil and butter, if necessary. Transfer chicken to a plate. ▼

4. Add balsamic vinegar to the skillet; increase heat to medium-high and cook, stirring, to loosen any browned bits from the bottom and sides of the skillet, about 1 minute.

5. Return chicken and pan juices to the skillet; reduce heat to low and turn medallions once or twice to baste them in the sauce.

6. Add cooked pasta to the skillet with the vegetables, tossing to combine; warm over low heat until heated through, about 4 minutes.

7. Transfer pasta and vegetables to a platter. Arrange the chicken medallions on the platter next to the pasta and vegetables; garnish with fresh basil leaves and lemon wedges. Serve immediately.

Choice Cuts

The term *scaloppine* refers to thin slices of meat that are usually breaded, then quickly sautéed. You can use other types of meats in this recipe, such as turkey, pork or veal.

Chef's Trick

Using a rolling pin instead of a meat pounder will help to avoid tearing the thin meat medallions.

Veggie Medley

Replace the onion and mushrooms in this recipe with your favorite vegetables. Try chopped eggplant and tomatoes or red peppers and olives.

■ **GOOD IDEA** Make a chicken parmigiana hero with the leftovers. Spread with mozzarella and tomato sauce; reheat and enjoy!

Variations

Quick Fix

For an easy dinner, cut chicken breasts into 1-inch cubes; sauté with garlic until browned and cooked through. Toss with the cooked vegetables and pasta.

Great Garnish

Give each place setting a twist! For each garnish, stack 3 thin lemon slices; cut halfway through to the center of the slices. Gently twist slices together.

Stuffed Chicken Parmesan

You Will Need

❧❧❧❧

FOR THE STUFFED CHICKEN

- **6** boneless, skinless chicken breast halves (about 3¾ pounds total)
- **½** cup bread crumbs
- **¼** cup grated Parmesan cheese
- **1** tablespoon plus ¼ teaspoon dried oregano, divided
- **4** ounces mozzarella cheese, cut into 12 slices
- **1** tablespoon prepared basil pesto
- **2-3** tablespoons olive oil
- **¼** teaspoon salt
- **⅛** teaspoon freshly ground black pepper
- **1** can (8 ounces) tomato sauce
- **½** cup shredded mozzarella cheese
- **1** pound linguine, cooked

SERVES 6

COOKING TIME
20-25 MINUTES

Kitchen Tips

You can "grate" Parmesan cheese using a food processor. Cut the cheese into 1-inch chunks; add to processor and pulse in 10-second increments until the cheese is the desired consistency.

STUFFING THE CHICKEN

1. Rinse chicken; pat dry with paper towels and arrange on a baking sheet. Cover with plastic wrap; freeze chicken until it begins to become firm, about 30 minutes. Coat a casserole dish with vegetable cooking spray. In a shallow dish or pie plate, combine bread crumbs, Parmesan and 1 tablespoon oregano.

2. Using a small sharp knife, slice partially through each chicken breast horizontally to create a deep pocket. ▼

3. Place 2 slices mozzarella in the pocket. Spread ½ teaspoon pesto over the cheese. ▼

4. Fold top of breast over stuffing, making sure cheese is covered. Repeat with remaining chicken breasts, cheese and pesto. Dredge each stuffed chicken in bread crumb mixture, coating both sides; reserve leftover crumbs. ▼

BAKING THE CHICKEN

1. Preheat oven to 350°F. In a large skillet, heat 2 tablespoons olive oil over medium heat. Add coated chicken to the skillet; cook until lightly browned, about 2 minutes per side.

2. Transfer chicken to the prepared casserole dish. Sprinkle with remaining oregano, salt and pepper. Pour tomato sauce over chicken; top with shredded mozzarella. Bake chicken until sauce is bubbly and meat springs back when touched with a fingertip, 20-25 minutes.

3. Meanwhile, transfer reserved bread crumbs to a small skillet. Toast crumbs over medium-low heat until browned, about 2 minutes.

4. To serve, divide warm linguine among 6 plates. Transfer a chicken breast to each plate; spoon sauce from casserole dish over each serving. Sprinkle browned bread crumbs over linguine.

It's Italian!

Italian cooks would call this chicken *alla parmigiana*. The phrase means "in the style of Parma," and often refers to any dish made with Parmesan cheese. Other popular *alla parmigiana* dishes are made with veal and eggplant.

Super Stuffer

You can easily change the stuffing to make other delicious dishes. For stuffed chicken Florentine, fill chicken breasts with spinach and grated Parmesan; or, stuff with Swiss cheese, mushrooms and ham for Chicken Cordon Bleu.

■ **GOOD IDEA** Add slices of prosciutto or cooked Italian sausage to the cheesy filling for a tasty surprise!

Variations

Purchased Pastas

Fresh and dried pastas are available in an array of shapes and flavors. For a change of pace, serve chicken Parmesan with fresh spinach linguine.

Italian-Style Breadsticks

For zesty bread, brush refrigerated breadstick dough with an egg wash seasoned with basil, garlic, oregano, pepper; top with mozzarella and bake.

"New" Chicken Saltimbocca

You Will Need

❦❦❦❦

FOR THE CHICKEN

4 boneless, skinless chicken breast halves (1½ pounds total)

4 slices ham

4 slices provolone cheese

4 fresh sage leaves, chopped

freshly ground black pepper

3 tablespoons all-purpose flour

2 tablespoons butter or margarine

4 cloves garlic, minced

2 cups prepared tomato sauce

1 cup red wine or chicken stock

FOR THE GARNISH

fresh sage leaves

SPECIAL AIDS

kitchen mallet or rolling pin

toothpicks

SERVES 4

COOKING TIME
15 MINUTES

Kitchen Tips

- The thinner you pound the chicken, the easier it is to roll.

- Substitute ¾ teaspoon dried sage for the chopped fresh sage leaves called for in this recipe.

PREPARING THE CHICKEN

1. Trim fat and tenders from chicken. Using a kitchen mallet or a rolling pin, pound chicken to an even thickness, taking care not to tear the meat. ▼

ASSEMBLING THE CHICKEN ROLLS

1. Place chicken on a work surface, smooth-side down; top each piece with 1 ham slice and 1 provolone slice. Divide sage among 4 pieces of chicken; season with black pepper to taste.

2. Roll up each piece and secure with a toothpick; dredge in flour. ▼

COOKING & SERVING THE CHICKEN

1. In a large skillet, melt butter over medium-high heat. Add chicken; cook, turning, until browned, about 3 minutes.

Stir in garlic; immediately add tomato sauce and wine. Bring mixture to a boil; reduce to a simmer and cover tightly. Cook, turning twice, until chicken is no longer pink, about 12 minutes longer.

2. Remove chicken from the skillet; remove the toothpicks and cut chicken rolls into ¾-inch slices. ▼

3. Pour sauce from the skillet onto each serving plate; top with sliced chicken. Garnish with fresh sage leaves; serve immediately.

Attention to Detail

As a side dish for this chicken dinner, serve this simple pasta:

PASTA WITH GARLIC & OLIVE OIL

¼ cup olive oil

2 cloves garlic, minced

1 tablespoon chopped fresh parsley

salt and pepper to taste

12 ounces cooked spaghetti, drained

¼ cup grated Parmesan cheese

In a small skillet, heat oil over low heat; add garlic and cook until softened. Add parsley, salt and pepper. Toss with pasta and Parmesan. Serves 4.

A New Classic

This rolled chicken saltimbocca is a novel variation on a classic Italian dish that uses veal. It got the name saltimbocca, which means "jump into the mouth," because it tastes so delicious.

Florentine Flair

Prepare this dish as they do in Florence: Place a layer of fresh spinach leaves on the chicken before adding the ham.

Casserole It

Layer cooked chicken and these fillings in a casserole dish, then bake at 375°F for 30 minutes.

GOOD IDEA Serve this dish with a simple pasta tossed with garlic and olive oil. Offer amaretto cookies and gelato for dessert.

Variations

One-Dish Dinner

For a full-course meal in a bowl, toss rigatoni, broccoli florets and marinara sauce. Add slices of chicken saltimbocca and serve.

Colorful Chicken Spirals

Combine Old World flavor with nouvelle-cuisine style. Roll the chicken with bright-red peppers and serve with a colorful salad.

Monte Cristo Sandwich

MAKING THE DIPPING SAUCE

1. In a small saucepan, combine honey and apple juice over medium heat; cook until simmering, about 2 minutes. Set aside dipping sauce.

ASSEMBLING THE SANDWICHES

1. Place 4 slices of bread on a cutting board. Top each slice with 2 slices turkey and 2 slices ham, folding to fit on bread. Top meat with another slice of bread. Add 2 slices of cheese to each sandwich, folding cheese to fit on bread. Sprinkle with salt and pepper to taste. Top cheese with remaining bread slices.

2. Using a sharp knife, cut off bread crusts. Slice each sandwich in half diagonally. ▼

3. Insert a toothpick into each half to secure.

COOKING THE SANDWICHES

1. Preheat oven to 250°F. In a small bowl, using a wire whisk, beat eggs and milk until combined. In a large nonstick skillet, melt 1 tablespoon butter over medium-high heat.

2. Dip 4 sandwich halves into the egg mixture, coating completely. ▼

3. Cook until browned on 1 side, about 2 minutes. Add 1 tablespoon butter to the skillet; remove toothpicks and turn sandwiches. Cook until browned on the other side, about 2 minutes longer. Transfer sandwiches to an ungreased baking sheet; place the sheet in the oven to keep warm. ▼

4. Repeat dipping and cooking process with remaining sandwiches.

SERVING THE SANDWICHES

1. Divide dipping sauce evenly among 4 small bowls. Serve each whole sandwich with 1 bowl dipping sauce.

Lunch Classic

This tasty sandwich combines the best of 2 worlds—lunch and breakfast! Slices of Swiss cheese, turkey and ham are grilled between thin layers of French toast.

Condiments

Classic Monte Cristos are accompanied by confectioners' sugar and jelly or a sweet sauce like this one. For a tart version, serve with mustard and sliced sweet pickles.

Savory Touches

Cook the sandwiches with a little garlic or add basil or spinach leaves to the layers.

GOOD IDEA Give your meal a taste of New England with a maple syrup sauce and an apple-cranberry-celery compote.

Variations

Sweet Monte Cristo

For breakfast or a filling snack, make a Monte Cristo sandwich with cream cheese and jelly.

Fruit Salad Side

A light, fresh salad of sliced fruit is all you need to turn this rich sandwich into a satisfying meal.

Cajun Blackened Catfish

You Will Need

✿✿✿✿✿

FOR THE SPICE BLEND

- 1 tablespoon ground allspice
- 1 tablespoon chili powder
- 1 tablespoon ground cumin
- 1 tablespoon garlic powder or garlic flakes
- 1 tablespoon black pepper
- 1 tablespoon white pepper
- 1 tablespoon dried rosemary
- 1 tablespoon dried thyme

FOR THE CATFISH

- 6 catfish fillets (about ½ pound each)
- 3-4 tablespoons vegetable oil
- 6 thick lemon slices

SERVES 6

COOKING TIME
9-11 MINUTES per batch

Kitchen Tips

- **When cooking catfish fillets of uneven thickness, start thick ones first, then add the thinner fillets so they will be done at the same time.**

- **You can remove the fishy smell from hands, utensils and work surfaces by rubbing them with lemon wedges.**

MAKING THE SPICE BLEND

1. In a blender or food processor fitted with a metal blade, combine allspice, chili powder, cumin, garlic powder, black pepper, white pepper, rosemary and thyme; pulse until spices are pulverized, about 1 minute.

MAKING THE CATFISH

1. Transfer about one-half of spice blend to a large plate. Using your fingers, rub each fish fillet lightly with oil. ▼

2. Dredge each fillet in spice blend. Add more spices to plate as necessary. ▼

3. In a large skillet, heat remaining oil over medium-high heat until almost smoking; add 2 fillets and cook for 1 minute. Turn fillets; immediately reduce heat to medium-low. Cook fillets, uncovered, until they flake slightly when pierced with a fork, 8-10 minutes. ▼

4. Transfer fillets to a serving platter; cover with foil. Continue cooking remaining fillets; garnish with lemon slices and serve immediately.

Attention to Detail

No Cajun dish is complete without this traditional accompaniment:

DIRTY RICE

- 1 pound ground beef
- 1 medium onion, chopped
- 1 green bell pepper, chopped
- 1 celery stalk, chopped
- 3 tablespoons vegetable oil
- salt and black pepper
- 1 cup long-grain rice
- 2½ cups water

1. Heat a large skillet over medium heat; add ground beef, onion, bell pepper, celery, oil and salt and pepper to taste; cook until beef is browned and crumbly, about 6 minutes.

2. Stir in rice. Add water; reduce heat and simmer, covered, until all water has been absorbed, about 30 minutes. Fluff rice with a fork; serve.

Hot Stuff

For a devilishly fiery dish, add 1 teaspoon cayenne pepper to this spice mix.

Personal Blend

Create your signature blackening blend by adding lemon pepper, onion powder, celery seeds, mustard seeds, crushed oregano or dried lemon zest to this recipe.

Choosing Fish

Let your nose be your guide when choosing fresh fish; avoid "fishy" odors. Look for firm, shiny skin and clear eyes on whole fish; avoid shriveled edges and dull flesh on fillets.

■ GOOD IDEA

Complete this Cajun dinner with a classic Southern dessert such as pecan pralines or sweet-potato pie.

Variations

Blackened Chicken

Add Creole style to your fried chicken. Mix equal amounts of blackening spices and flour; dredge chicken before frying.

Spicy Gift

Make a double batch of this spice blend and give some to a friend or fishing buddy. Be sure to include this Cajun catfish recipe with your gift.

Bread Bowl Chili

You Will Need

FOR THE BREAD BOWL

 1 large round bread loaf

FOR THE CHILI

 1 medium jalapeño pepper, diced

 12 ounces lean ground beef

 2 teaspoons olive oil

 2 medium yellow onions, chopped (about 2 cups)

 1 medium green bell pepper, chopped (about 1 cup)

 1 tablespoon chili powder

 1 can (14½ ounces) whole tomatoes

 ¼ cup no-salt-added tomato paste

 1 can (8½ ounces) red kidney beans, drained and rinsed

 1 can (7 ounces) whole kernel corn, drained

SERVES 4

**COOKING TIME
40 MINUTES**

Kitchen Tips

Once you serve the chili, slice the bread bowl into wedges and serve. The flavor of the chili gives the bread an added zest.

MAKING THE BREAD BOWL

1. Using a serrated knife, slice off about an inch from the top of the bread.

2. Carve out a "bowl" from within the bread, leaving about 1 inch inside. ▼

MAKING THE CHILI

1. To chop jalapeño pepper, use a knife and fork to hold in place. Chop pepper into fine pieces. Avoid touching seeds with your hands. ▼

2. In a large nonstick skillet, cook beef over medium heat, stirring, until browned, about 5 minutes. Drain beef.

3. In same skillet, heat oil over medium heat. Add onions; cook, stirring, for 5 minutes. Add bell pepper, jalapeño pepper and chili powder; cook, stirring, for 5 minutes.

4. Add beef, tomatoes with liquid and tomato paste; bring to a boil. Reduce heat to low; simmer for 25 minutes. Add beans and corn; cook 5 minutes longer.

5. Ladle chili into bread bowl and serve immediately. ▼

Attention to Detail

Another popular dish to serve in a bread bowl is Creamy Spinach Dip. The inside of the bread is cubed and served alongside the dip.

CREAMY SPINACH DIP

 1 cup frozen chopped spinach, thawed and drained

 1 cup sour cream

 ½ cup cottage cheese

 1 tablespoon dried onion flakes

 1 teaspoon lemon juice

 salt and pepper to taste

Combine all ingredients in a large bowl. Chill for 2 hours. Return to room temperature before serving.

Bread Tips

Choose a hearty bread that feels heavy for its size. Pumpernickel raisin, corn rye or sour-dough bread are good choices. If the texture of the bread is too soft, the chili will be absorbed too quickly.

Serving Idea

Serve this chili as a winter warmer lunch. Make the chili the night before. Reheat just before you are ready to serve. Along with a dollop of sour cream, garnish the chili with shredded cheddar cheese and chopped cilantro.

■ **GOOD IDEA** For extra spice, add $1/4$ teaspoon of cayenne pepper to the chili when simmering.

Variations

Simply Chili

Of course, this chili can also be served without the bread bowl. Serve the chili over rice or noodles to make a complete meal.

A Great Duo

Fill a bread bowl with your favorite chunky beef stew. The bread will absorb some of the flavor of the stew, making for a great accompaniment.

Beef Stew with Polenta

You Will Need

🌿🌿🌿

FOR THE POLENTA

- **2** packages (2 pounds) instant polenta
- **½** cup all-purpose flour
- **½** cup (1 stick) butter

FOR THE STEW

- **5-6** tablespoons olive oil, divided
- **4** medium onions, coarsely chopped (about 3 cups)
- **2** medium cloves garlic, sliced
- **2** pounds small white button mushrooms
- **4** pounds lean beef chuck, cut into ¾-inch cubes
- **1** cup all-purpose flour
- **2** teaspoons sugar
- **1** cup red wine or tomato juice
- **1** cup water
- **2** teaspoons herbes de Provence or ½ teaspoon each dried thyme, basil, rosemary and marjoram
- **2** whole bay leaves
- **1** teaspoon salt
- **1** package (10 ounces) frozen green peas

SPECIAL AIDS

8 coffee mugs or 4 drinking glasses
resealable plastic bags

SERVES 8

COOKING TIME
1 HOUR 30 MINUTES plus chilling

PREPARING THE POLENTA

1. Prepare polenta according to package directions, using the method given for "firmer" polenta. While polenta is cooking, line 8 coffee mugs (or 4 tall straight-sided drinking glasses) with plastic bags. When polenta is ready, pour into lined mugs, smoothing out any air pockets. Chill until polenta is set and holds its shape when bag is pulled from mug, at least 1 hour or overnight. ▼

MAKING THE STEW AND POLENTA

1. In a large heavy skillet, heat 3 tablespoons oil over low heat. Add onions; sauté until translucent, but not browned, about 10 minutes. Add garlic; sauté 1 minute longer. Transfer onions and garlic to a plate, leaving oil in skillet. Add 2 tablespoons oil; add mushrooms, tossing to coat. Cook over medium heat, stirring frequently, about 5 minutes; transfer mushrooms to plate with onions.

2. Dredge beef cubes in flour; shake off excess. In skillet, cook beef in small batches over high heat until brown on all sides, about 6 minutes per batch, adding more oil, if necessary. Return all beef cubes to skillet. Add sugar;

cook, stirring, until sugar caramelizes slightly, about 1 minute. ▼

3. Add wine and water to skillet; boil over high heat, stirring, for 1 minute. Reduce heat to low; add cooked onions and mushrooms, herbs, bay leaves and salt. Cover; cook, stirring occasionally, until meat is tender, about 45 minutes. Remove bay leaves. Add peas and cook, covered, 10-15 minutes longer.

4. Unmold polenta from the mugs and remove the plastic bags. ▼

5. Slice polenta into ½-inch rounds; dust with flour. In a skillet, heat butter over medium-low heat. Add polenta; cook until golden, about 3 minutes. Serve with stew.

About Polenta

Polenta consists only of cornmeal, salt and water, but it is quite time-consuming to make from scratch. Using instant polenta saves time and it tastes just as good. Or, try prepared polenta logs, either plain or in a flavor that goes well with the recipe.

True Grit

Cornmeal is ground into 3 textures: fine (often called corn flour); medium (the most common grind); and coarse (also known as polenta).

GOOD IDEA Serve polenta for breakfast on a cold morning. It's a treat topped with butter and maple syrup or brown sugar.

Variations

Try Polenta

Add variety to your menus with polenta instead of rice or potatoes. Its rich corn taste pairs well with robust sauces and grilled meats and vegetables.

Mulled Apple Cider

Entice guests with the spicy-sweet aroma of this cider. Simmer 2 quarts fresh cider, 1 teaspoon whole cloves and 2 cinnamon sticks for 15 minutes.

Cider-Glazed Pork Medallions

You Will Need

❧❧❧❧

FOR THE PORK MEDALLIONS

- 1   quart apple cider
- 4   sprigs fresh rosemary, divided
- 2   bay leaves
- ¾   teaspoon salt
- ½   teaspoon freshly ground black pepper
- 4   boneless pork loin chops, ½ inch thick (about 1½ pounds)
- 3   tablespoons butter or vegetable oil, divided
- 1   medium onion, thinly sliced (about ½ cup)
- 2½   medium cloves garlic, minced (about 1¼ teaspoons)
- 2   tablespoons Dijon-style mustard
- 1½   tablespoons cornstarch
- 1   apple, julienned

SPECIAL AIDS
kitchen mallet

SERVES 4

**COOKING TIME
30 MINUTES**

Kitchen Tips

- If you don't have a kitchen mallet or tenderizer, use the bottom of a heavy saucepan or an unopened coffee can.
- When purchasing pork, look for meat that is pink, not gray or red. External fat should be smooth and white, not chalky or discolored.

MAKING THE PORK MEDALLIONS

1. In a small saucepan, combine cider, 2 sprigs rosemary and bay leaves. Bring to a boil over high heat; cook until mixture is reduced to about 2 cups, about 12 minutes. Remove and discard rosemary sprigs and bay leaves.

2. Remove leaves from remaining rosemary and chop finely; discard stems. In a small bowl, combine chopped rosemary, salt and pepper.

3. Trim fat from pork. Place each chop between 2 sheets of waxed paper. Using a kitchen mallet, pound the chops firmly to a ¼-inch thickness. ▼

4. Season both sides of chops with rosemary mixture.

5. In a large skillet, melt 1 tablespoon butter over medium-high heat. Add onion and garlic; cook until tender, about 3 minutes. Add onion and garlic to cider mixture.

6. In the same skillet, melt remaining butter. Add pork chops; cook over high heat until browned and tender, about 3 minutes per side. ▼

7. In a small bowl, combine mustard and cornstarch; stir into cider mixture.

8. Pour cider mixture over pork chops in skillet and cook over high heat until sauce is thickened, about 2 minutes. Add apple, stirring to coat. ▼

9. Reduce heat to medium; cover and cook until apple is heated through, about 5 minutes.

Perfect Pair

Apple and rosemary make a delicious duo! Look for other ways to pair these flavors. Sprinkle chopped rosemary over baked apples or apple crisp. Or, add it to the batter for apple muffins.

Scent-erpiece

For an aromatic table arrangement, place pillar candles in a basket; surround with polished apples and sprigs of rosemary.

Flavor Change

For a switch, smother the pork medallions with a combination of mustard, garlic, honey and fresh thyme.

GOOD IDEA For a fragrant napkin ring, cut sprigs of rosemary into 3-inch lengths and tie around rolled napkins.

Variations

Rosemary Applesauce

For a sophisticated twist on a classic side dish, simmer applesauce with fresh rosemary for 30 minutes; strain through a mesh sieve.

Harvest Salad

Apples add sweet flavor to any salad. Arrange apple slices over fresh greens; sprinkle with toasted nuts, crumbled blue cheese and a balsamic vinaigrette.

Cranberry Pork Chops

You Will Need

❧❧❧❧

FOR THE PORK CHOPS

- 2 tablespoons all-purpose flour
- ¼ teaspoon freshly ground black pepper
- 4 center-cut loin pork chops (about 6 ounces each), trimmed
- 2 teaspoons olive oil

FOR THE RELISH

- 2 medium apples, cored and coarsely chopped
- 2 tablespoons water
- ¼ cup sugar
- 1 package (12 ounces) cranberries
- 2 teaspoons cornstarch
- ½ teaspoon ground sage
- ⅓ cup balsamic vinegar or red-wine vinegar

SERVES 4

COOKING TIME
30 MINUTES

Kitchen Tips

- Before using cranberries, discard any that are soft, discolored or shriveled; pluck off any stems.

- To broil pork chops, coat with mustard and bread crumbs. Broil chops 5 inches from heat, turning once until cooked through, about 6 minutes per side.

PREPARING THE PORK CHOPS

1. On a sheet of waxed paper, combine flour and pepper; mix well. Dredge pork chops in the flour mixture, tapping off excess and turning to coat. ▼

2. In a large nonstick skillet, heat oil over medium heat. Add pork chops and cook, turning once until cooked through, about 15 minutes.

3. Make a small slit in the thickest part of the meat, or near the bone, and check the color. Chops should be light gray and no longer pink. ▼

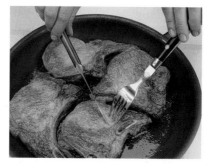

PREPARING THE RELISH

1. In a small saucepan, combine apples, water and sugar. Cook, over low heat, until soft, about 15-20 minutes.

2. In a small bowl, combine cranberries, apple mixture, cornstarch and sage. Mix well.

3. Heat a large skillet over medium heat. Add cranberry mixture. Cook, stirring constantly until cranberries soften, about 2 minutes. Add vinegar to skillet. Cook, stirring, until mixture thickens, about 10 minutes. ▼

4. Spoon relish into a bowl. Garnish with a sprig of sage, if desired. Serve with pork chops.

Attention to Detail

Don't rely simply on lemon wedges and fresh parsley for platter garnishes. Assorted fresh fruit serve as both a colorful presentation as well as tasty side bites.

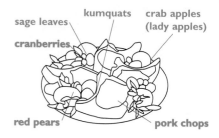

sage leaves — kumquats — crab apples (lady apples)

cranberries

red pears — pork chops

Apple Idea

Try sugar-glazed apples for a great side dish. Slice 2 medium cooking apples, such as Winesap or Cortland, into wedges. (There is no need to peel the apples.) In a skillet over medium heat, cook apple wedges with 1 teaspoon sugar, stirring, until they are just tender, about 3 minutes.

Great Gift

For a thoughtful gift, spoon the prepared cranberry relish into a fancy jar and attach a homemade label and a recipe for the pork chops.

GOOD IDEA For added sweetness, combine a 16-ounce can of sliced cling peaches, drained and chopped, with the relish.

Variations

Flavor Enhancer

The sweet tangy taste of the cranberry relish makes a great accompaniment to any roasted chicken, turkey or ham dinner.

Southwestern Garnish

The cranberry relish dresses up lean pork chops to make a low-fat easy-to-prepare midweek dinner. Pork loin is a lean alternative to fattier red meats.

Dilled Pork Dijonaise

You Will Need

❦❦❦❦❦

FOR THE DIJON-DILL BUTTER

- 1 tablespoon butter, softened
- 1 tablespoon Dijon-style mustard
- 1 tablespoon chopped dill
- ¼ teaspoon grated lemon zest

FOR THE PORK

- 4 ½-inch-thick boneless loin pork chops (about 5 ounces each)
- 1 tablespoon olive oil
- 2 cloves garlic, peeled and smashed
- ⅛ teaspoon black pepper
- ⅛ teaspoon salt
- lemon wedges
- sprigs of dill

SPECIAL AIDS
kitchen mallet

SERVES 4

COOKING TIME
5 MINUTES

Kitchen Tips

Avoid overcooking this cut of meat to keep it from being dry. To check for doneness, remove a pork chop from the skillet and make a small slice in the center. When pork is done, it will be very slightly pink.

MAKING THE DIJON-DILL BUTTER

1. In a small bowl, combine butter and mustard; stir until a paste consistency is reached. Stir in dill and lemon zest until thoroughly combined; set aside. ▼

MAKING THE PORK

1. Place pork chops between sheets of waxed paper. Using a kitchen mallet, pound each pork chop to a ¼-inch thickness. ▼

2. In a large nonstick skillet, heat oil over medium-high heat. Add garlic, then pork chops, pushing garlic aside so it is not underneath meat. Sprinkle pork chops with pepper and salt. Cook for 2 minutes; turn pork chops over.

3. Divide butter mixture evenly over the 4 chops, spreading to coat. ▼

4. Continue cooking pork chops until cooked through, about 3 minutes longer. Transfer to a serving platter; spoon any pan juices over pork chops. Garnish pork with lemon wedges and dill sprigs; serve immediately.

Attention to Detail

FLAVORED BUTTER

This technique of quickly sautéing thin cuts of meat with flavored butter can be adapted to your own tastes. Try making herbed butter with one of these flavor combinations and use it on pork or veal scallops or thinly pounded chicken breasts:

- sage and honey mustard
- rosemary and garlic
- parsley and lemon

Quick Dinner

This recipe is perfect when you need a last-minute dinner—the pork chops are ready in under 10 minutes!

Go-Withs

For a complete meal, serve these chops on a bed of baby greens with roasted potatoes and steamed green beans with almonds.

Piquant Sides

The Dijon-dill butter in this recipe adds life to so many ordinary side dishes: Stir it into mashed potatoes; add it to pureed rutabaga, turnips or carrots; or, just spread it onto hot dinner rolls.

GOOD IDEA Dress your table in the flavors of the meal. Use lemon-colored linens and a fresh dill bouquet.

Variations

Flavorful Butter

You can double, triple or quadruple this butter recipe for later use in dozens of dishes. Just roll it in waxed paper and freeze.

Dijon Veal Scaloppine

For another delicious dinner classic, replace the pork with veal scallops. These thinly pounded veal cutlets require about half the cooking time.

Basic Roasting

You Will Need

❧❧❧❧

FOR THE HERBED RIB ROAST

- 1   standing rib roast (about 6 pounds)
- 1   large clove garlic, halved
- 1   teaspoon each dried thyme, crushed rosemary, dry mustard powder and black pepper
- ½   teaspoon salt

SPECIAL AIDS

meat thermometer

1. Preheat oven to 450°F. In a large roasting pan, place roast on its ribs, fat side up; rub with garlic.

2. In a small bowl, combine thyme, rosemary, dry mustard, pepper and salt; rub mixture on roast. Insert thermometer in center of roast, making sure it does not touch the bone.

3. Roast meat for 25 minutes. Reduce heat to 300°F; continue cooking until thermometer registers 150°F-155°F for medium doneness, about 1 hour 45 minutes. Remove from oven; let stand 15-20 minutes before carving.

SERVES 6

SEASONING THE ROAST
First, rub fresh garlic on the meat; then combine the other seasonings and rub the mixture into the roast. The meat will absorb the flavors as it cooks.

CHECKING THE TEMPERATURE
A meat thermometer will tell you when the roast is done to your liking. When you insert it in the roast, make sure it doesn't touch the bone.

CARVING A RIB ROAST
Place a finished rib roast on its side to make it easier to carve. Using a sharp carving knife, slice toward the bone; cut along the rib to remove each slice.

REMOVING THE RIBS
It will be easier to continue slicing a rib roast if you remove the ribs along the way. Cut along the bottom edge of the rib to free it from the roast.

MAKING GRAVY
Use beef broth to deglaze the roasting pan over medium heat; add some flour to the gravy to thicken. Strain through a fine mesh sieve for a smooth result.

ROASTING VEGETABLES
Root vegetables, such as potatoes, are best for roasting. Toss with vegetable oil and season as desired. Stir occasionally during the roasting process.

Roasting utilizes dry heat to sear the outside of the meat, leaving the inside tender, moist and flavorful.

There are many opinions about meat roasting techniques. Some cooks suggest using high temperatures for a short time; others advocate lower temperatures with longer cooking times. Still others prefer a combination of the two methods. Any method will produce a tender, juicy, flavorful addition to the dinner table! Roasting has even become a popular way to enhance the flavor of vegetables, such as garlic, onions, potatoes and other root vegetables.

Once you have followed these basic tips for roasting, you will come to learn which methods work best for you.

Tools of the Trade

BASIC EQUIPMENT
A heavy-duty roasting pan keeps meat from burning. Some cuts need a rack and baster. Finish gravy with a separator or sieve, and carve with a sharp carving knife.

SEASONING SAVVY
To flavor the meat before roasting, rub on various spices, such as dry mustard, thyme or rosemary, coarsely ground black pepper and fresh garlic.

For Best Results

- To ensure that the meat cooks evenly, let the meat sit at room temperature for about 1 hour before roasting.

- Pat the meat dry before cooking; too much moisture can affect its texture.

- The best beef cuts for roasting are top or bottom round, top sirloin and eye of round.

How to Stuff a Roast

You Will Need

FOR THE ROAST
1 butterflied half-shank leg of lamb (5-6 pounds) or 1 butterflied boneless rolled rump roast (3-3½ pounds)
2-3 tablespoons vegetable oil

FOR THE STUFFING
2 cups prepared bread or rice stuffing

SPECIAL AIDS
meat mallet
kitchen twine
instant-read thermometer

1. Using a mallet, pound meat to a 2½-inch thickness.
2. Spread stuffing over meat. Starting from 1 side, roll meat over stuffing. Tie the rolled roast at 2-inch intervals with kitchen twine.
3. Preheat oven to 350°F. In a heavy-bottomed roasting pan, heat vegetable oil over medium-high heat. Add roast; brown on all sides, 6-8 minutes. Transfer roast, seam-side down, to a wire rack set in the roasting pan.
4. Roast meat, uncovered, until instant-read thermometer registers 155°F-165°F, 1 hour 45 minutes-2 hours. Remove roasting pan from oven; let roast stand for 15 minutes before carving.

SERVES 6

POUNDING THE MEAT
To tenderize and flatten meat, pound it with the rough, or macerated, side of a meat mallet. Strike at an angle to prevent tearing the meat.

CHOOSING A STUFFING
A stuffing can include just about any ingredients you like. The key is bread or bread crumbs, which absorb the flavors and juices from the meat.

ROLLING THE ROAST
Beginning at 1 side, roll the meat over the filling to form a tight, neat bundle. Make sure the stuffing is completely covered at all edges.

TYING THE STUFFED ROAST
To tie a roast, lay lengths of twine at 2-inch intervals vertically on the work surface. Lay the rolled roast across the twine; tie twine securely around roast.

TESTING FOR DONENESS
Insert an instant-read thermometer into the thickest part of the meat—not into the stuffing! Wait 20 seconds for the temperature to register accurately.

RESTING THE ROAST
When the roast has reached its final temperature, remove it from the oven and let it stand for at least 15 minutes to allow the juices to distribute.

Before you roast a large cut of meat, add a flavorful stuffing—and create a new taste sensation.

Roasting meat really brings out its flavor and juices. When a hearty stuffing is added, the flavors penetrate the meat—and a whole new dish is created! This technique is especially useful for less expensive cuts of meat, which might need a boost of flavor or texture.

Using the basic tools found in almost every kitchen, it's easy to stuff and roll a roast. Don't worry about deboning the roast to prepare it for stuffing; you can buy cuts of meat that are already deboned and butterflied. Or, look for a ready-rolled roast at your supermarket or butcher; then just fill it with your favorite stuffing, roast and slice!

Tools of the Trade

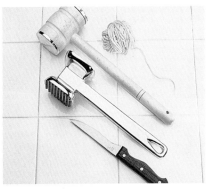

BACK TO BASICS
The tools needed for stuffing include a sharp knife, a metal or wooden meat mallet for tenderizing the meat and kitchen twine for tying the rolled roast.

TAKING TEMPERATURES
An instant-read thermometer is the best tool for reading the roast's temperature. It is inserted toward the end of cooking time to check for doneness.

For Best Results

• **Choose a roasting pan that is not much larger than the roast. This will keep the pan drippings from burning and ruining the meat's flavor.**

• **Moisten the surface of the meat mallet with cooking oil or water to keep it from sticking to the meat.**

• **Leave a thin layer of fat on the roast; it keeps the meat juicy.**

Rib Roast Dinner

MAKING THE POTATOES

1. Preheat oven to 400°F. Pierce potatoes several times with a fork. Bake until tender, about 1 hour. Meanwhile, melt butter in a large nonstick skillet set over medium heat. Add peppers and onion; sauté until tender, about 5 minutes. Add ham; sauté for 5 minutes.

2. Reduce temperature to 350°F. Cool potatoes slightly. Slice tops off potatoes and scoop out pulp; reserve skins. In a bowl, mash pulp. Stir in 1 cup Colby, milk, sour cream and vegetable mixture. Spoon mixture into potato shells.

3. Sprinkle potatoes with remaining Colby. Place on baking sheet. Bake until heated through, about 20 minutes. Serve with roast.

MAKING THE ROAST

1. Increase oven temperature to 425°F. Rub the pepper evenly over beef, pressing gently so pepper adheres.

2. Place the herbs in a large measuring cup and chop using kitchen shears. ▼

3. On a sheet of waxed paper, combine fresh and dried herbs. Roll beef in herb mixture to completely coat. ▼

4. Loosely tie the beef at 2-inch intervals with kitchen twine. Place beef on roasting rack. ▼

5. Roast until an instant-read meat thermometer registers 155°F. for medium, about 30 minutes. Let stand for 5 minutes; carve into thin slices.

Attention to Detail

Use a meat thermometer to check the doneness of the beef.

For rare	130°F
For medium	155°F
For well-done	170°F

Leftover Idea

Leftover roast beef will keep for up to 2 days in the refrigerator. Cover the meat tightly with plastic wrap.

Menu Idea

Along with hearty double-stuffed potatoes, serve the beef with steamed baby carrots in a dill butter sauce.

Make Ahead

Prepare and stuff potatoes up to 1 day in advance. Wrap in plastic wrap and refrigerate until ready to bake.

GOOD IDEA Use leftover roast beef to make hearty sandwiches for the next day's lunch.

Variations

An Appetizer to Please
Stuff small red potatoes instead of the russets and serve them as a snack or appetizer. They are delicious!

A Tasty Idea
Substitute large sweet potatoes for the russets. Try Monterey Jack cheese on top instead of Colby.

Perfect Prime Rib

You Will Need

FOR THE PRIME RIB

1 bone-in rib roast
(3¹/₂-4 pounds)
freshly ground black pepper

FOR THE SAUCE

3 tablespoons butter
or margarine, melted
and divided

1 cup sliced white button
mushrooms

1¹/₂ tablespoons all-purpose
flour

2 tablespoons red-
wine vinegar

1 cup dry red wine or
beef broth

1 bay leaf

2 cups beef broth

SPECIAL AIDS

meat thermometer

SERVES 6

**COOKING TIME
1 HOUR 15 MINUTES**

Kitchen Tips

You can still roast a prime
rib even if you don't own
a meat thermometer.
Roast the prime rib a total
of 20-22 minutes per pound
for medium doneness.

ROASTING THE PRIME RIB

1. Preheat oven to 425°F. Set a roasting rack over a 13- x 9-inch baking pan.

2. Sprinkle sides of roast liberally with pepper. Insert a meat thermometer into the center of the roast; place roast on the rack. Roast for 25 minutes.

3. Reduce heat to 325°F. Continue roasting until the thermometer registers 140°F-150°F for medium doneness, 45-50 minutes longer, checking the temperature frequently after 30 minutes.

4. Transfer roast to a cutting board; cover loosely with foil and let stand for 15 minutes. Set roasting pan aside.

MAKING THE SAUCE

1. In a small skillet, heat 1¹/₂ tablespoons butter over medium-high heat. Add mushrooms and sauté until browned, about 4 minutes. In a small bowl, mix remaining butter and flour until well blended; set aside.

2. Pour off drippings from the baking pan, reserving 2 tablespoons; return reserved drippings to the pan.

3. Place the pan over medium heat. Add vinegar, wine and bay leaf; bring to a boil. Using a wooden spatula, scrape browned bits from bottom and sides of pan. Boil sauce until reduced to ¹/₂ cup, about 5 minutes. Add beef broth; continue boiling sauce until reduced to 2 cups, about 5 minutes longer. Remove and discard bay leaf; pour sauce into a small saucepan.

4. Add flour mixture to sauce and whisk until smooth and slightly thickened, about 3 minutes. Add mushrooms, stirring to combine.

CARVING THE PRIME RIB

1. Cut a thin slice off 1 end of roast to make a level surface; stand roast cut-side down. ▼

2. Steady roast with a carving fork. Slice horizontally toward rib; make a vertical cut along rib to remove slice. Remove the rib bones, one at a time, with a horizontal cut as you carve off the slices. Serve prime rib with sauce. ▼

Beauty Sleep

Letting your roast "rest" after it has finished cooking will help redistribute its moisture, making the meat juicier and easier to carve.

British Dish

To round out your prime-rib dinner, try a Yorkshire pudding. This British bread dish is delightfully easy to make and is the traditional side dish for prime rib.

Prime Lunch

Turn leftover beef and sauce into open-faced sandwiches. Serve on thick cuts of warm French bread.

GOOD IDEA Don't wait for a holiday to enjoy this feast. It's perfect for homecomings and other celebrations.

Variations

Steak-House Staple

A baked potato topped with a dollop of sour cream and some chopped fresh chives is a great prime-rib side dish. Start the potatoes 15 minutes after the roast.

Family Favorite

Your dinner would not be complete without a classic green bean casserole. Generously coat cooked green beans with melted butter, then toss with crunchy slivered almonds.

Beef Wellingtons

Kitchen Tips

Look for the puff pastry in the freezer section of the supermarket. It usually takes several hours to thaw, so plan accordingly.

MAKING THE BEEF WELLINGTONS

1. In a small bowl, combine egg and milk; set aside.

2. In a large skillet, melt butter over medium-high heat; add steaks. Cook, turning once, until browned on both sides, about 5 minutes per side. Transfer steaks to a platter; pat dry with some paper towels.

3. On a lightly floured surface, roll out each pastry dough sheet to a ¼-inch thickness. Cut each sheet in half.

4. Place a steak in the center of each pastry piece. Fold pastry over steak. ▼

5. Trim excess dough; pinch ends to seal. Brush with egg mixture. ▼

6. Roll out dough trimmings. Using a leaf-shaped cookie cutter, cut out leaves. Place leaves on top of pastry; brush with remaining egg mixture. Place steaks on a baking sheet in the freezer for 30 minutes. ▼

7. Preheat oven to 425°F. Bake wrapped steaks until pastry is golden and puffed, about 20 minutes for medium-rare. Transfer to serving plates.

MAKING THE BEARNAISE SAUCE

1. In a small bowl set over simmering water, combine vinegar, 2 teaspoons tarragon and pepper. Bring mixture to a boil; cook until reduced by half.

2. Gradually beat in egg yolks. Cook until slightly thickened, about 2 minutes. Remove from heat.

3. Add butter in a thin stream, whisking constantly until mixture thickens. Stir in remaining tarragon. Serve along with Beef Wellington.

Warming Tip

If the Bearnaise sauce is ready before the Beef Wellington, keep it warm in a double boiler or in a metal bowl set over hot, not boiling, water.

Meal Ideas

Puff pastry is easy to work with and provides flaky results every time. You can wrap many foods in puff pastry for an elegant, yet easy meal. Instead of the steaks, try grilled vegetables, poached chicken, ground beef, lamb steaks or even a seafood medley.

■ **GOOD IDEA** Beef Wellington makes a great entrée for a winter holiday meal. It is easy to prepare, yet elegant to present.

Variations

Make a Show

Wrap a cooked tenderloin roast in puff pastry and bake until puffed and golden. Serve sliced to reveal the delicious beef within.

Bearnaise Sauce

A Bearnaise sauce is the classic accompaniment to Beef Wellington. It is a very rich sauce that complements the tender beef well.

Steak Pinwheels

You Will Need

FOR THE STEAK AND FILLING

- 1 flank steak (about 1¾ pounds)
- 2 teaspoons red-wine vinegar
- 1 large egg, beaten
- ¾ cup dry-packed sun-dried tomatoes, soaked in hot water and chopped
- ¼ cup grated Parmesan cheese
- 1 medium yellow or red bell pepper, chopped (about ¾ cup)
- 2 green onions, chopped
- ⅔ cup bread crumbs

SPECIAL AIDS

kitchen twine or string

SERVES 6

COOKING TIME
12-15 MINUTES

Kitchen Tips

To cut meat easily, use the right knife. The best type has a very flexible, long (usually 10-inch) blade. Make sure it's sharp for the cleanest cuts.

PREPARING THE PINWHEELS

1. Preheat oven to 400°F. Line a baking sheet with foil. Using a sharp knife, cut steak horizontally into two thin layers. Rub cut sides of meat with vinegar. ▼

2. In a medium bowl, combine egg, sun-dried tomatoes, Parmesan, bell pepper, green onions and bread crumbs.

3. Place 1 steak on cutting board and spread half of the filling on top, leaving 1 inch uncovered on long sides. Roll steak from long end. Tie at 1¼-inch intervals with kitchen twine. ▼

4. Slice steak between strings; place cut-side up on prepared baking sheet. Repeat with remaining meat and filling. ▼

5. Bake pinwheels 12-15 minutes for medium doneness. Remove twine before serving.

Attention to Detail

Fluffy rice pilaf goes well with this dish. Add any herbs you have on hand.

BASIC RICE PILAF

- ¼ cup (½ stick) margarine
- 1 teaspoon salt
- 2 cups long-grain white rice
- 4 cups water
- ¼ cup (½ stick) butter, diced

In a large saucepan, melt margarine over medium-high heat; add salt and rice. Sauté until rice is golden, about 8 minutes; add water. Boil until water is absorbed, about 10 minutes. Stir in butter. Cover, reduce heat to low and cook until rice is tender, stirring occasionally, about 10 minutes.

Make it Tender

For a truly tender piece of flank steak, cut the steak in half horizontally and pound each piece with a meat mallet. Roll with stuffing and cook to rare or medium rare (flank steak cooked to medium or well done can become tough).

Twice is Nice

You can use the filling for this dish in any number of creative ways. Try adding ¼ cup olive oil and tossing with curly pasta for a meal that's thrifty and simple to prepare.

GOOD IDEA Serve this dish family style on a large platter. Drizzle with a red pepper sauce for a dramatic touch.

Variations

On the Side

This filling is so flavorful, it can stand on its own as a side dish with your favorite cut of steak. Serve it with fish and poultry dishes, too.

Summer Filling

During summer, when basil is plentiful, substitute fresh pesto for the filling. Add bread crumbs and shredded mozzarella cheese for a seasonal taste treat.

Lamb Chops with Potato Stars

You Will Need

❦❦❦❦

FOR THE LAMB

- 2 rib racks of lamb, trimmed (about 1½ pounds each)
- 1 tablespoon Dijon-style mustard
- 2 tablespoons chopped fresh rosemary
- 2 tablespoons chopped fresh parsley
- 2 shallots or ¼ red onion, finely chopped (about 2 tablespoons)
- ½ teaspoon crushed dried thyme
- ½ teaspoon salt

FOR THE POTATOES

- 4 large potatoes (about 2 pounds)
- 1 tablespoon olive oil

FOR THE ASPARAGUS

- 24 spears asparagus (about 1½ pounds)

SPECIAL AIDS

2-inch star cookie cutter

SERVES 4

BAKING TIME
1 HOUR 20 MINUTES

Kitchen Tips

A rack of lamb has 4-6 ribs each. To serve 4 people, ask your butcher for racks with at least 4 ribs.

COOKING THE LAMB CHOPS

1. Preheat oven to 400°F. Score the fat on the lamb in a crisscross fashion.

2. Cover exposed rib ends with foil and rub lamb with mustard. ▼

3. In a small bowl, combine rosemary, parsley, shallots, thyme and salt; sprinkle on lamb. Place lamb in a shallow baking pan; bake for 35-40 minutes.

COOKING THE POTATOES

1. Slice potatoes lengthwise into ⅜-inch pieces. Using a 2-inch star cookie cutter, cut out shapes. ▼

2. Toss potatoes with oil and place in baking pan around lamb. Continue baking until lamb is medium (150°F. on an instant-read thermometer) and potato stars are golden, about 40 minutes longer. Cover and let stand 10 minutes.

COOKING THE ASPARAGUS

1. Clean asparagus, trimming off tough stem ends, if necessary. Place in a large skillet with 2 cups water. Cover and bring to a boil; simmer 5-10 minutes, until asparagus is just tender.

SERVING THE DISHES

1. Using a sharp knife, cut rack of lamb between ribs to form chops. ▼

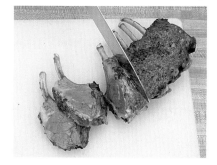

2. Place 2 chops on each individual plate. Serve the lamb chops with potato stars and asparagus.

Attention to Detail

For a kid-friendly meal, arrange the potato stars and asparagus spears to look like shooting stars. Children are delighted by decorative food, and they just might eat their vegetables!

Cooking Tip

Lamb is a wonderfully delicate meat and is best served slightly pink. Stick to the cooking times to keep it tender.

Herbal Touch

Fresh rosemary is a sure sign of spring. Its aromatic flavor goes particularly well with lamb—use it liberally

Home-Grown

American lamb, raised in every state of the Union, is preferred to the imported product because the cuts are larger and meatier. Domestic lamb is usually grain fed and has a milder flavor.

GOOD IDEA Lamb is a traditional symbol of spring. Serve it with other springtime classics, like new potatoes and asparagus.

Variations

Star Quality

Add some of the cooked potato stars to your favorite lamb stew—it will make a decorative and nutritious meal that's fun to eat.

Star Kebabs

For lamb kebabs, skewer cubed lamb, thick slices of boiled potato stars, cherry tomatoes and zucchini cubes. Brush with your favorite marinade.

Stuffed Pork Tenderloins

You Will Need

❧❧❧❧❧

FOR THE STUFFING

1/4 cup (1/2 stick) butter or margarine

2 cups dried bread crumbs

1 medium yellow onion, diced (about 1 cup)

1 medium red bell pepper, diced (about 1 cup)

FOR THE TENDERLOIN

1 pork tenderloin, trimmed (about 1 pound)

1 roasted red bell pepper, cut into thin strips

SPECIAL AIDS

kitchen string

SERVES 4

COOKING TIME
25 MINUTES

Kitchen Tips

● **Arrange the stuffing in center of the tenderloin and roll up tightly. Be careful not to overstuff the tenderloin. Leaving a 1/2-inch border will prevent the stuffing from spilling out.**

● **After tying the tenderloin with kitchen string at 2-inch intervals, tie more string around the tenderloin lengthwise, end to end.**

MAKING THE STUFFING

1. In a large skillet, melt butter over medium heat. Add bread crumbs, onion and bell pepper; stir until golden.

MAKING THE TENDERLOIN

1. Preheat broiler. Line broiler pan with foil; spray with vegetable cooking spray.

2. Make a 2-inch-deep cut along the long side of pork, without cutting all the way through. Spread pork flat.

3. Spread stuffing down center of pork, leaving a 1/2-inch border. Arrange roasted peppers over stuffing. ▼

4. Starting with a short end, tightly roll up pork. ▼

5. Tie stuffed pork with kitchen string at 2-inch intervals. Place pork in prepared broiler pan. ▼

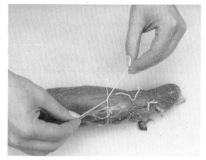

6. Broil pork, turning occasionally, until an instant-read thermometer inserted in the center registers 160°F., about 25 minutes.

7. Transfer pork to a carving board and let stand for 10 minutes. Slice pork; serve immediately.

Attention to Detail

Try this easy side salad:

ASPARAGUS SALAD

1 tablespoon lemon juice

2 tablespoons olive oil

2 teaspoons minced shallots

salt and pepper, to taste

3/4 pound asparagus, trimmed, cut diagonally into 1 1/2-inch pieces and blanched

8 cherry tomatoes, halved

In a large bowl, whisk together lemon juice, olive oil, shallots and salt and pepper; add asparagus and tomatoes. Toss to coat. Chill before serving.

Choosing Pork

When purchasing pork tenderloin, be sure the lean part is firm and fine-textured and grayish pink to light red in color.

Buffet Delight

Because it's generally served cut into medallions, pork tenderloin is a good dish to serve at a buffet. Roasted red potatoes and a green vegetable, such as asparagus, are great side dishes for pork.

Garnish Tip

Fragrant parsley sprigs are a beautiful garnish for this dish.

GOOD IDEA

To save time, use a packaged stuffing mix. Stuff and roll tenderloin as recipe directs.

Variations

Fruit Stuffing

Substitute dried apricots and dried cranberries for the onion and bell pepper. Fruit adds a delicious touch of sweetness to the pork.

Easy Pork Chops

If you prefer, serve pork chops rather than a tenderloin. Place a spoonful of stuffing on top of each chop and bake as usual.

Asian Style Pork Roast

You Will Need

❦❦❦❦

FOR THE PORK ROAST

1   2-pound boneless pork roast

FOR THE MARINADE

juice of 4 medium limes (about ½ cup)

½   cup soy sauce

2   green onions, minced (about ⅓ cup)

3   tablespoons brown sugar

2   tablespoons minced fresh cilantro

2   tablespoons toasted sesame oil

2   cloves garlic, minced (about 1 tablespoon)

1   tablespoon minced fresh gingerroot

1   teaspoon black pepper

½   teaspoon hoisin sauce or 1 tablespoon apricot jam (optional)

¼   teaspoon crushed red pepper flakes

FOR THE GARNISH

2   tablespoons plum sauce

1   cup snow pea pods, blanched

2   fresh apricots or 4 canned apricot halves

SPECIAL AIDS

large resealable plastic bag
13- x 9-inch roasting rack
meat thermometer

SERVES 4

COOKING TIME
1 HOUR PLUS MARINATING

PREPARING THE PORK AND MARINADE

1. Rinse pork roast with cold water; pat dry with paper towels. ▼

2. Place pork in a large resealable plastic bag; set aside. In a small bowl, combine lime juice, soy sauce, green onions, brown sugar, cilantro, sesame oil, garlic, gingerroot, black pepper, hoisin sauce and red pepper flakes. Stir until sugar is dissolved.

3. Pour marinade into the plastic bag with pork; seal the bag and turn to coat pork completely with marinade. ▼

4. Chill pork and marinade, turning once or twice, for at least 1½ hours or overnight.

ROASTING THE PORK

1. Preheat oven to 450°F. Place a roasting rack in a 13- x 9-inch roasting pan; transfer pork to the rack. Insert a meat thermometer in the thickest part of pork; spoon half of marinade over top.

2. Roast pork for 10 minutes; baste with some of the remaining marinade. Reduce the oven to 350°F; continue roasting, basting occasionally with the remaining marinade, until the meat thermometer registers 160°F, about 50 minutes longer. Let pork stand for 15 minutes before slicing.

GARNISHING AND SERVING THE PORK

1. To serve, spoon about 2 tablespoons plum sauce onto the center of a small serving platter.

2. Cut pork into ¼-inch slices; arrange slices on the platter in an overlapping semicircle around plum sauce.

3. Arrange snow pea pods, in a pile, to complete the circle of meat. Cut each apricot into wedges. Place overlapping apricot wedges in the center. ▼

Versatile Pork

Pork can be used in so many ways! Whether you serve spareribs at barbecues or tender medallions sautéed with wine and herbs for an elegant dinner, it makes great meals.

Just Ducky

Also known as "duck sauce," plum sauce is a thick, sweet-and-sour condiment made with plums, apricots, sugar and seasonings.

Summer Supper

For a summertime meal, roast the pork ahead and chill it well. Serve on a platter with colorful vegetable and fruit garnishes.

■ **GOOD IDEA** To give this meal an authentic Asian touch, start with tender vegetable dumplings or crisp spring rolls.

Variations

Sesame-Crusted Roast

Flavor your roast with the slightly sweet taste of sesame. Press $^1/_4$-$^1/_2$ cup toasted sesame seeds onto the meat just before putting it into the oven.

Pork Stir-Fry

You'll love these leftovers. Slice extra pork into $^1/_4$-inch strips and stir-fry with garlic, ginger, bell peppers and onions. Add soy sauce and serve over rice.

Spinach-Stuffed Pork Chops

You Will Need

❧❧❧

FOR THE PORK CHOPS

- 4 1-inch-thick pork chops (about 8 ounces each)
- ½ teaspoon paprika
- ½ teaspoon salt

FOR THE STUFFING

- 1 tablespoon olive oil
- ½ red onion, chopped (about ½ cup)
- 1 stalk celery, chopped (about ½ cup)
- ⅔ cup chopped mushrooms
- 1 teaspoon chopped garlic
- 1 package (10 ounces) frozen chopped spinach, thawed and squeezed dry
- ½ cup chicken broth or water
- 2 slices whole-wheat bread, cut into small cubes (about 1½ cups)
- ⅛ teaspoon ground sage

SERVES 4

COOKING TIME 30-35 MINUTES

Kitchen Tips

When shopping for pork, choose cuts that are pale pink with white (not yellow) fat. The darker the coloration, the older the meat.

PREPARING THE PORK CHOPS

1. Preheat oven to 400°F. Grease an 11- x 7-inch baking dish. Using a sharp, thin-bladed knife, split the chops lengthwise on one side to make a pocket. Leave other sides intact. ▼

MAKING THE STUFFING

1. In a medium skillet, heat oil over medium-high heat; add onion, celery and mushrooms. Cook until softened, about 8 minutes. Stir in garlic, spinach and broth. Reduce heat; simmer about 3 minutes. ▼

2. Remove stuffing mixture from heat; lightly stir in bread and sage until combined.

STUFFING THE PORK CHOPS

1. Spoon stuffing into pork chops. Be careful not to overstuff, since stuffing will expand while baking. ▼

2. Using an offset spatula, place chops in prepared baking dish; sprinkle with paprika and salt.

3. Bake stuffed pork chops until juices run clear when meat is pierced with a fork, 30-35 minutes.

Attention to Detail

After thawing frozen spinach, squeeze the water out to prevent the stuffing from becoming soggy. You can do this by hand or by pressing spinach against the inside of a colander with a wooden spoon; then place spinach on paper towels to absorb any excess moisture.

Sautéing Tip

Fresh mushrooms naturally contain water, so stir them constantly to help cook off moisture. Excess liquid results in a weaker flavor.

Choosing Chops

When selecting pork chops for stuffing, choose cuts that are 1-2 inches thick. If you don't have time to prepare the chops, ask your butcher to cut pockets in them.

Simple Sauce

Make a glaze from pan drippings; drizzle it over the chops and serve the remainder in a gravy boat.

GOOD IDEA For a special touch, serve these chops with homemade applesauce seasoned with cinnamon and nutmeg.

Variations

Chicken Stuffer

Use this filling to stuff 4 boneless chicken breasts. Bake at 350°F. until juices run clear, about 25 minutes.

Tasty Side Dish

You'll want to make this stuffing as a companion to other meats. Substitute 2 cups packaged mix for the bread and double the other ingredients.

Fancy Roast Chicken Dinner

You Will Need

FOR THE ROAST CHICKEN

- 3 cups seasoned bread stuffing
- 1 roasting chicken (about 7 pounds)
- 1 teaspoon salt
- 1 teaspoon black pepper

FOR THE ROAST GARLIC

- 4 tablespoons melted butter
- ¼ cup olive oil
- 3 heads of garlic

FOR THE VEGETABLE BUNDLES

- 1 large carrot
- 1 pound green beans, steamed
- 1 bunch green onions, stalks only, blanched

SERVES 6

**ROASTING TIME
2 HOURS**

Kitchen Tips

- To steam green beans, bring a little water to a boil in a large saucepan. Place green beans in a steamer basket and place basket in pan. Steam, covered, just until tender, about 5 minutes.

- To blanch green onion stalks, plunge stalks into boiling water until they become limp, about 5 seconds. Plunge into ice water and drain.

ROASTING THE CHICKEN

1. Preheat oven to 350°F. Prepare stuffing according to package directions. Sprinkle chicken with salt and pepper. Spoon stuffing into cavity. Tie legs together.

2. Place chicken on rack in a roasting pan. Roast until meat thermometer inserted in thickest part of thigh registers 180°F., about 2 hours.

ROASTING THE GARLIC

1. To roast the garlic, in a small bowl, combine butter and olive oil. Cut garlic heads in half; do not peel.

2. Brush butter mixture over cut garlic heads. Place garlic on a small baking sheet. Roast alongside chicken. ▼

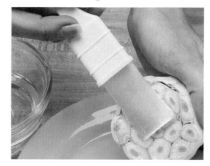

MAKING THE VEGETABLE BUNDLES

1. Fill a medium bowl with ice water. Using a vegetable peeler, or a sharp paring knife, peel carrot into very thin strips. In a small saucepan, bring water to boil.

2. Drop carrot strips into boiling water until they become limp, about 10 seconds. Remove strips and plunge into ice water; set aside. ▼

3. Gather some green beans; wrap a carrot strip around each bunch and tie with blanched green onion stalk. ▼

SERVING THE CHICKEN

1. Transfer chicken to a serving platter; let stand for 15 minutes before carving. Transfer stuffing to a serving bowl.

2. Arrange green bean bundles around chicken. Place roasted garlic heads on a decorative plate.

Time Saver

Cook the chicken without stuffing and cut down on cooking time. Make a quick stove-cooked stuffing to serve on the side.

Make Ahead

Use your favorite stuffing recipe and make it ahead of time. Place cooled stuffing in a bowl. Cover the bowl with plastic wrap and refrigerate for up to 2 days.

Best Steaming

When steaming vegetables, make sure you have a tightly-sealed lid to ensure even cooking.

▪ GOOD IDEA

Serve a refreshing sorbet or sherbet for an easy dessert.

Variations

Company Fare

For a change of pace, serve 3 roasted Cornish hens that have been filled with stuffing.

Garlic Spread

Roast some extra garlic and refrigerate in an air-tight container to use as a spread for toasted bread slices.

Honey Mustard Chicken

You Will Need

FOR THE CHICKEN

  4 skinless, boneless chicken breast halves (4 ounces each)

FOR THE SAUCE

  1 jar clover honey

  3 tablespoons white-wine vinegar or cider vinegar

  1 tablespoon dry mustard

  2 tablespoons chopped green onions

  1 teaspoon Dijon-style mustard

  $\frac{1}{2}$ teaspoon dried thyme

  $\frac{1}{4}$ teaspoon dried oregano

FOR THE GARNISH

lemon wedges

herb sprigs

SPECIAL AIDS

honey dipper

SERVES 4

**BAKING TIME
30 MINUTES**

Kitchen Tips

It's important to make sure that the poultry is thoroughly cooked. To check for doneness on chicken breasts, use a meat thermometer and insert it horizontally into center of the breast. The thermometer should read about 180°F.

PREPARING THE CHICKEN

1. Rinse chicken with cold water and pat dry with paper towels. Place chicken on a cutting board. Using a sharp knife, lightly score chicken breasts on both sides. ▼

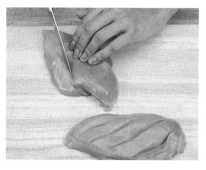

MAKING THE SAUCE

1. Preheat oven to 400°F. Line a baking pan with foil. Spray foil with nonstick vegetable cooking spray.

2. Using a honey dipper, measure out $\frac{1}{4}$ cup honey. ▼

3. In a small bowl, stir together vinegar and dry mustard. Add honey, green onions, Dijon-style mustard, thyme and oregano. Mix well.

BAKING THE CHICKEN

1. Place chicken in prepared pan. Brush chicken with half of honey mustard sauce.

2. Bake, turning once and brushing with remaining sauce, until chicken is cooked through and no longer pink, about 30 minutes.

3. Place chicken on a serving platter. Garnish with lemon wedges and herb sprigs. ▼

Attention to Detail

Try using different types of honey in this recipe. Always be aware of the strength of the flavor before trying to make the substitution.

Clover: mild-tasting and most common type; best for general cooking

Pure Orange Blossom: light and delicate with a citrus taste

Manuka: from New Zealand; rich-tasting and good for cooking

Money Saver

A great way to save money is to buy whole chickens or parts on sale and freeze them for future meals.

Easy Prep

Spray a measuring cup with nonstick vegetable cooking spray before adding the honey. This will make cleanup a snap.

Make Ahead

Prepare the honey mustard sauce in advance. Place sauce in an airtight plastic container and store in the refrigerator for up to 1 week.

GOOD IDEA The honey mustard sauce makes a great dip for chicken nuggets.

Variations

A Gift for the Hostess

For a thoughtful gift, offer a jar of honey and a jar of mustard in a decorative basket with a recipe for the sauce.

One Chicken for All

Use the honey mustard sauce on chicken parts and please both the dark- and white-meat lovers in your family.

Chicken and Stuffing Casserole

You Will Need

FOR THE CHICKEN

1 tablespoon vegetable oil
4 whole chicken legs, cut at joint

FOR THE STUFFING

2 medium onions, chopped (about 1 cup)
2 stalks celery, chopped (about 1 cup)
2 packages (16 ounces each) frozen cubed butternut squash
1 medium red bell pepper, chopped (about 1 cup)
1 cup chicken broth
1 large egg
1¼ teaspoons poultry seasoning
1 teaspoon salt
8 cups cubed stale wheat bread (about 12 slices)
½ cup chopped fresh parsley

SERVES 8

**BAKING TIME
60-70 MINUTES**

Kitchen Tips

• If the stale bread is not completely dried out, spread the cubes evenly on a baking sheet. Bake at 250°F. until dry, about 15 minutes; cool.

• For the most accurate reading when testing for doneness, insert the thermometer so the stem does not touch the bone.

PREPARING THE CHICKEN

1. Preheat oven to 350°F. Grease a 13- x 9-inch casserole dish. In a large skillet, heat oil over medium heat until hot but not smoking. Add chicken legs and cook, turning until all sides are golden, about 12 minutes; set aside. ▼

MAKING THE STUFFING

1. Pour off all but 1 tablespoon of fat from skillet; return to heat. Add onions and celery; cook 5 minutes, stirring occasionally. Add squash and bell pepper and cook until softened, about 5 minutes longer. Transfer to a large bowl. ▼

2. Stir in broth, egg, poultry seasoning and salt. Add bread cubes and parsley; mix well.

3. Place mixture into prepared dish. Place chicken pieces on top. ▼

BAKING THE CASSEROLE

1. Bake until chicken juices run clear when pierced with a fork or, if using a thermometer, when internal temperature reaches 180°F., 60-70 minutes.

Attention to Detail

Searing adds color to the chicken and enriches the flavor. To sear meat:

• Heat a heavy skillet over high heat until a little water added to the pan beads and evaporates on contact.

• Reduce the heat to medium; add enough oil to coat the skillet bottom and swirl to cover.

• When oil is hot enough to sizzle chicken on contact, add legs in a single layer and cook, turning, until they turn a rich golden brown.

• Chicken will appear seared on the outside but will still be rare on the inside and need further cooking.

cook's essentials step-by-step cookbook

Aromatic Flavor

For a mild, almost sweet anise flavor, substitute fennel for the celery and add a teaspoon of ground fennel seed to the stuffing. Use fresh fennel greens for a fragrant garnish.

No Bones

Remove chicken from bones to make eating easier. Or better yet, ask your local butcher to bone the chicken when you buy it.

Go-With

Just as with turkey, the tart flavor of cranberry sauce goes great with this dish.

GOOD IDEA Host a family dinner to celebrate the autumn harvest. Serve this casserole and fresh apple pie for dessert.

Variations

Chicken Again?

No! But you still can enjoy the stuffing. Just substitute 8 small pork chops for the chicken and add a cup of cooked, crumbled sausage to the stuffing.

Thanksgiving Every Day

Why wait for a holiday to enjoy a whole roasted bird? Prepare a small, 3 1/2-pound chicken with stuffing for a hearty meal.

Mexican Casserole

You Will Need

❧❧❧❧❧

FOR THE CASSEROLE

8 ounces orecchiette or other small-size pasta

1 tablespoon vegetable oil

2 cloves garlic, minced

1 medium red onion, chopped (about 1 cup)

1 medium green bell pepper, chopped (about 1 cup)

2 cups shredded cooked chicken

1 can (11 ounces) corn kernels, drained

1 can (4½ ounces) chopped green chilies, drained

1 cup whole milk ricotta cheese

1 cup shredded Monterey Jack cheese, divided

½ teaspoon chili powder

1½ cups salsa, divided

FOR THE TOPPING

3 flour tortillas

2 tablespoons vegetable oil

chopped green onions

SERVES 6

**BAKING TIME
20 MINUTES**

Kitchen Tips

Salsas come in various degrees of heat, usually mild, medium and hot. Use one that your whole family can enjoy.

MAKING THE CASSEROLE

1. Preheat oven to 375°F. Cook pasta according to package directions; drain.

2. Heat oil in a skillet over medium heat; add garlic, onion and bell pepper. Cook, stirring frequently, until tender, about 5 minutes. In a large bowl, combine pasta, vegetable mixture, chicken, corn, chilies, ricotta cheese, ½ cup Monterey Jack and chili powder.

3. Spoon some salsa in the bottom of a medium casserole dish. Spoon chicken mixture over salsa. Top with more salsa and sprinkle evenly with remaining cheese. Bake casserole until mixture is heated through, about 20 minutes. ▼

MAKING THE TOPPING

1. Stack tortillas and slice them into ½-inch strips. ▼

2. Heat oil in a large skillet over medium heat. Cook the tortilla strips until lightly golden, about 5 minutes. Transfer to a paper towel to drain. ▼

3. Spoon any remaining salsa in center of casserole. Top with tortilla strips and sprinkle with chopped green onions.

Attention to Detail

It's party time, and you can make your table look even more special with just a few quick and easy table accessories:

● A small cactus is very inexpensive and can give a Mexican look to your table.
● Serve tortilla chips in clean terra-cotta flower pots or bowls.
● Play some Mexican mariachi music to complete the mood.

Make Ahead

To make this tasty casserole in advance, prepare it as the recipe directs, but do not bake. Cover with plastic wrap and refrigerate for up to 1 day. Bake as recipe directs.

Lighten Up

Rather than whole milk ricotta cheese, substitute part-skim ricotta cheese.

Money Saver

Any leftover meats, such as shredded cooked turkey or cooked ground beef, can be used to fill this casserole.

■ **GOOD IDEA** For more heat, add a chopped and seeded jalapeño pepper.

Variations

Mexican Fiesta Dinner

This recipe doubles as a filling for tortillas and taco shells. Simply omit the pasta and top with fresh salsa, sour cream and herbs or guacamole.

Delicious Dip

For an easy appetizer, reserve ½ cup of the chicken mixture from the casserole recipe, omit the pasta and toss with 1 cup salsa. Serve with tortilla chips.

Meat Loaf Roll-Up

You Will Need

❧❧❧❧❧

FOR THE STUFFING

4	slices bacon, chopped
2	stalks celery, chopped
1½	cups frozen corn kernels
⅔	cup hot water
2⅔	cups corn bread stuffing mix (from an 8-ounce package), divided
¼	cup chopped fresh parsley

FOR THE MEAT LOAF

2	pounds ground beef
2	eggs
½	cup barbecue sauce, divided
¼	cup milk
1	tablespoon dried minced onion or toasted onion
¼	teaspoon salt
¼	teaspoon black pepper

SPECIAL AIDS

instant-read thermometer

SERVES 8

**BAKING TIME
50 MINUTES**

Kitchen Tips

Some markets sell "meat loaf mix," a blend of ground beef, pork and veal. This blend will work well in this recipe.

MAKING THE STUFFING

1. In a large skillet, cook bacon over medium-high heat for 5 minutes. Stir in celery; cook until celery is tender and bacon is crisp, about 5 minutes longer.

2. Add corn and water to the skillet; cook until water boils. Remove skillet from heat. Stir in 2 cups corn bread stuffing mix and parsley; set aside.

MAKING THE MEAT LOAF

1. Preheat oven to 350°F. Spray a large rectangular baking dish with vegetable cooking spray.

2. In a large bowl, thoroughly combine remaining stuffing mix, ground beef, eggs, ¼ cup barbecue sauce, milk, dried onion, salt and pepper.

3. On a large sheet of waxed paper or aluminum foil, shape meat mixture into a 12- x 10-inch rectangle. Spread stuffing mixture evenly over meat loaf to within 1 inch of the edges. ▼

4. Starting at 1 short end and using the waxed paper to lift the edges, roll up meat loaf, jelly-roll style. ▼

5. Pinch the seams and edges to seal. Using your hands, press loaf firmly to hold the shape; transfer to the prepared baking dish.

6. Bake loaf for 45 minutes. Brush top with the remaining barbecue sauce; continue baking loaf until it registers 160°F on an instant-read thermometer, about 5 minutes longer. Let meat loaf stand 5 minutes before slicing.

Attention to Detail

To give your meat loaf a new flavor, substitute any of the following liquid ingredients for the barbecue sauce:

- sweet-and-sour sauce
- chutney
- soy sauce
- fruit or vegetable juices
- fruit puree or apple butter

Veggie Boost

It's simple to sneak a little extra nutrition into this meal—just sauté some favorite veggies along with the celery and bacon. Try chopped spinach, mushrooms, peppers, carrots or zucchini.

Quick Loaf

If you're in a hurry, just crumble crispy bacon directly into the meat mixture and bake in a traditional shape.

Layered Loaf

Create a new look for this recipe: In a loaf pan, alternate layers of corn bread stuffing with this tasty meat loaf mixture.

GOOD IDEA Mix up a blend of barbecue sauce and ketchup as a condiment for this dinner. Spike it with cayenne, if you dare.

Variations

Super Sides

For a colorful and tasty meal, round out this dinner with some spicy, thick-cut fries and a refreshing orange, avocado and red onion salad.

Make Mine an MLT

Got leftovers? Make a meat loaf, lettuce and tomato sandwich! Serve it with barbecue sauce on whole-wheat or your favorite bread.

Lasagna Sausage Rolls

You Will Need

❧❧❧❧❧

FOR THE LASAGNA SAUSAGE ROLLS

- 12 Italian sausage links (about 2½ pounds), grilled or pan-fried
- 1 pound lasagna noodles
- 2 teaspoons olive oil
- 1 red bell pepper, julienned
- 1 green bell pepper, julienned
- 1 pound ricotta cheese
- 2 eggs, lightly beaten
- ½ teaspoon freshly ground nutmeg
- ¼ teaspoon freshly ground black pepper
- 4 cups chunky Italian-style tomato sauce, divided
- 1 cup shredded mozzarella cheese (about 4 ounces)
- 24 large fresh basil leaves

SERVES 6

BAKING TIME 45 MINUTES

Kitchen Tips

- To remove the lasagna rolls from the pan, slide two large serving spoons down the sides of the roll; lift straight up.
- Avoid adding oil to the pasta cooking water or moistening the ends of the noodles; the noodles will be slippery and difficult to seal.

PREPARING THE LASAGNA SAUSAGE ROLLS

1. Slice off rounded ends from grilled sausages; discard. ▼

2. Cook noodles as package directs, removing from heat 2 minutes before suggested cooking time. Drain noodles and spread on a kitchen towel to cool slightly, about 5 minutes.

3. In a medium skillet, heat oil over medium heat. Add bell peppers; sauté until slightly softened, about 3 minutes. Transfer peppers to a plate; set aside oil in skillet to cool to room temperature.

4. In a medium bowl, combine ricotta, eggs, nutmeg and black pepper; stir well.

5. Grease the sides of a 9- or 10-inch round baking dish with reserved oil; cover the bottom of the baking dish with about 1 cup tomato sauce.

MAKING THE LASAGNA ROLLS

1. Preheat oven to 350°F. Spread each noodle with ¼ cup ricotta mixture, leaving a 1-inch border at 1 end; sprinkle mozzarella over ricotta mixture. Top with peppers and basil. ▼

2. Place 1 sausage crosswise over filled end of each noodle; wrap noodle around sausage and roll to within 3 inches of unfilled end. Bring unfilled end of each noodle up to seal. ▼

3. Stand each lasagna roll on end in the prepared baking dish. Top each lasagna roll with about 1 tablespoon tomato sauce; spoon remaining sauce into the baking dish between lasagna rolls and around edges. Bake lasagna rolls until heated through but not browned, about 45 minutes.

Lasagna Verde

Lasagna isn't always red! Make it green with spinach lasagna noodles and a filling of sautéed spinach, then top with pesto.

Laid Back

For a different look, lay rows of lasagna rolls on their sides in a rectangular pan and spread tomato sauce over the tops.

Try Tomatoes

Thinly sliced tomatoes are a delicious switch from the peppers in this filling. Roll them into each noodle with some chopped black olives and provolone and ricotta cheeses.

■ **GOOD IDEA**
Prepare heat-and-eat dinner servings by wrapping each roll in waxed paper and freezing in an airtight container.

Variations

Veggie Rolls

Make it a meatless meal. Roll noodles and filling around pieces of fresh zucchini with the ends trimmed. Bake as recipe directs.

It's a Toss-Up

Is this savory mixture better in lasagna rolls or simply tossed with a bowl of noodles? Try it both ways and let your family decide.

Beef Stir-Fry Wraps

You Will Need

❧❧❧❧❧

FOR THE MEAT AND MARINADE

- 1 flank steak (about 1 pound), partially frozen
- 3 tablespoons soy sauce
- 2 tablespoons mirin or seasoned rice vinegar
- 1 tablespoon canola oil
- 1 tablespoon cornstarch
- 1 tablespoon minced green onions
- ½ tablespoon minced jalapeño pepper
- 1 teaspoon dried lemon grass or ½ teaspoon lemon juice
- 1 teaspoon sugar

FOR THE FILLING

- 2 tablespoons canola oil
- 3 carrots, julienned
- 1 bunch green onions, cut into ½-inch pieces
- 1 zucchini, julienned
- 2 teaspoons minced fresh gingerroot
- 1½ tablespoons mirin or seasoned rice vinegar

FOR THE WRAPS

- 12 6-inch flour tortillas or rice-paper wrappers
- ½ cup hoisin sauce

SPECIAL AIDS
wok or large skillet

SERVES 6

COOKING TIME
8 MINUTES plus marinating

MARINATING THE STEAK

1. On a cutting board, cut steak into ⅛-inch-thick slices. Transfer steak to a medium nonreactive bowl.

2. In a small bowl, combine soy sauce, mirin, canola oil, cornstarch, green onions, jalapeño pepper, lemon grass and sugar. Pour marinade over steak; toss to coat completely. ▼

3. Cover steak with plastic wrap; let stand at room temperature for 1 hour.

MAKING THE FILLING

1. In a wok or large skillet, heat oil over medium-high heat. Add steak and cook until browned on all sides, about 4 minutes. Using a slotted spoon, transfer steak to a plate; set aside.

2. Add carrots to the wok. Using a wooden spoon, cook carrots, stirring constantly, for 1 minute. Add green onions; cook, stirring, for 1 minute longer. Add zucchini and gingerroot; cook, stirring, for 2 minutes longer.

3. Add mirin to the vegetable mixture; stir to blend. ▼

4. Return steak to the wok; cook until flavors are blended and meat is heated through, about 1 minute longer.

ASSEMBLING THE WRAPS

1. Stack tortillas between layers of paper towels; microwave on MEDIUM until softened, about 15 seconds. Spread 2 teaspoons hoisin sauce on 1 tortilla; top sauce with ½ cup filling. Fold sides of tortilla over filling. ▼

2. Continue with remaining tortillas, sauce and filling; serve.

Cross-Cultural

Drawing on a variety of culinary traditions, this recipe combines Mexican ingredients with Asian cooking techniques.

Wow Wraps

For an authentic Asian meal, substitute rice-paper wrappers for the tortillas and use an assortment of Chinese vegetables such as pea-pod strips, bok choy and sliced water chestnuts.

Sauce Notes

In China, hoisin sauce is used as an everyday condiment. Mirin is a low-alcohol, sweet rice wine used frequently in Japanese cuisine.

■ **GOOD IDEA** Make these as appetizers: Roll wraps tightly, cut into pieces and fasten with toothpicks. Serve in a lacquered box.

Variations

Chopstick Slaw

This spicy salad is great with Asian food. Toss sliced napa cabbage with shredded carrots, green onions, toasted sesame seeds, soy sauce, oil and mirin, a rice wine.

Asian Tacos

Can't decide between Mexican and Chinese? Spoon this beef filling into taco shells and top with shredded Chinese cabbage and hoisin sauce mixed with sour cream.

Classic Sausage Lasagna

You Will Need

- 1 box (16 ounces) lasagna noodles
- 2 large eggs
- 2 pounds ricotta cheese
- 2 cups shredded mozzarella cheese (8 ounces), divided
- ¼ cup grated Parmesan cheese
- 1 tablespoon dried basil
- ½ teaspoon salt
- 1 pound sweet or hot Italian sausage
- 1 medium onion, chopped
- 2 cloves garlic, minced
- ½ teaspoon crushed red pepper flakes
- 1 jar (48 ounces) tomato sauce
- 1 jar (6 ounces) roasted red peppers, drained and sliced

SERVES 8

**BAKING TIME
1 HOUR**

1. Preheat oven to 350°F. Cook lasagna noodles according to the package directions; drain in a colander and separate on a clean kitchen towel.

2. In a large bowl, combine eggs, ricotta, 1 cup mozzarella, Parmesan, basil and salt; mix well. Set aside. ▼

3. Remove sausage from casings. In a large nonstick skillet over medium-high heat, cook the sausage and chopped onion until browned, about 10 minutes, breaking up meat with a fork and adding the garlic and red pepper flakes during the last 2 minutes. Remove skillet from heat. Drain off fat.

4. Spread 1 cup tomato sauce in a 13- x 9-inch baking dish; layer with ⅓ of the noodles. Cover with half of the cheese mixture; top with half of the sausage. ▼

5. Arrange half of pepper slices over the sausage. Cover with 2 cups of sauce. Repeat layering with ⅓ noodles, cheese mixture, sausage, peppers and 2 cups of sauce. Top with a layer of noodles and the remaining sauce.

6. Sprinkle the reserved 1 cup mozzarella cheese on top. Bake the lasagna, covered with a sheet of aluminum foil, for 45 minutes. Uncover; bake until bubbly, about 15 minutes. Let stand for 5 minutes before serving.

Attention to Detail

- Lasagna noodles can stick together while cooking. Use plenty of water so they stay separated and aren't crowded. Start stirring as soon as you put them into the pot.

- To keep the noodles from becoming mushy during baking, boil them just until tender and drain quickly.

Light and Lean

For a healthier vegetarian version, chop 2 yellow squash and 2 zucchini and cook them with the onion instead of the sausage in step 3.

Easy Serving

Removing the first slice from a pan of lasagna is can be tricky. For best results, be sure to let it stand for 5 minutes and use a cake server or thin spatula.

Do Ahead

Lasagna can be assembled a day in advance or just hours before it's baked. For refrigerated lasagna, add at least 10 minutes to the baking time.

GOOD IDEA Make the meal complete with marinated mushrooms and artichokes, crusty bread or breadsticks and a fruit tart.

Variations

A Healthy Touch

Add wholesome goodness to lasagna by mixing 1 cup of cooked diced carrots or zucchini into the store-bought sauce. Add 1 teaspoon of your favorite dried herb for extra flavor.

Rosemary Twists

Savory breadsticks are a great go-with! Cut prepared bread dough into strips; twist and brush with a mixture of garlic, rosemary and olive oil. Bake at 350°F until golden brown, 10-15 minutes.

Penne, Shrimp & Tomatoes

You Will Need

FOR THE SAUCE

- 4 medium beefsteak tomatoes (about 2 pounds)
- 8 fresh basil leaves
- 2 cloves garlic, crushed
- ¼ cup extra-virgin olive oil
- 1 teaspoon balsamic vinegar
- ½ teaspoon salt
- ¼ teaspoon freshly ground black pepper

FOR THE PASTA AND SHRIMP

- 1 package (1 pound) penne pasta
- 12 ounces large frozen cooked shrimp, thawed (about 20 shrimp)

FOR THE GARNISH

- 1 sprig fresh basil
- grated Romano cheese (optional)

SERVES 6

PREPARATION TIME
20 MINUTES

Kitchen Tips

- Use your salad spinner to wash and dry your favorite herbs, just as you would for lettuce.
- The starch from the pasta cooking water adds moisture and thickness to the sauce.

PREPARING THE TOMATOES AND THE BASIL

1. Cut ¼ inch off top of 1 tomato; gently squeeze to remove seeds, using your finger to scoop, if necessary. Repeat with remaining tomatoes. ▼

2. Using a serrated knife, coarsely chop tomatoes. Working with 4-6 leaves at a time, roll basil from stem to tip; using a sharp knife, cut into thin strips. ▼

MAKING THE SAUCE

1. In a large bowl, combine tomatoes, basil, garlic, oil, vinegar, salt and pepper. Stir sauce until well blended; set aside.

SERVING THE PASTA

1. Cook pasta according to package directions. Set aside ¼ cup pasta cooking water. Transfer pasta to a colander. Run pasta under cool water; drain well. Stir reserved pasta cooking water into tomato sauce.

2. Line a serving bowl with shrimp. Add pasta to the center of the bowl; top with sauce. ▼

3. Garnish pasta with basil sprig and serve with Romano, if desired.

Attention to Detail

KEEPING BASIL IN THE KITCHEN

You can keep leftover fresh basil for several days in a jar filled with water. Place the jar in a sunny spot on the windowsill and pick the leaves off as you need them.

For long-term storage, blanch and freeze the leaves or puree the basil with a little olive oil and freeze it in ice-cube trays. To store, place frozen leaves or cubes of puree in freezer bags.

Olive Oil

Choose a good olive oil—like extra-virgin olive oil, which has a wonderful aroma and adds a distinct olive flavor to foods. Look for oil of the greenest color; the greener the color, the better the quality and flavor.

Herbal Delight

Substitute any of your favorite fresh herbs in this recipe—oregano, marjoram or parsley.

Saucy Fish

Use this fresh tomato sauce over cooked white fish, such as cod. Top with shredded mozzarella, then broil until cheese is melted.

GOOD IDEA Serve this meal hot for a weekday dinner. The next day, you can take leftovers to work for a great pasta lunch!

Variations

Scallop Switch

Try using sautéed sea or bay scallops instead of the shrimp in this recipe. Replace the penne with curvy pasta such as bow ties or shells.

Seaside Salad

Here's a cool pasta salad for a hot day: tuna with red bell peppers, radishes, cucumbers and pitted black olives, served on a bed of romaine lettuce.

Mediterranean Shrimp Melt

You Will Need

✦✦✦✦✦

FOR THE SHRIMP MELT

- 1 loaf (about 12 ounces) Italian bread, cut in half horizontally
- ¼ cup (½ stick) butter or margarine
- ¼ teaspoon garlic powder
- ¼ cup grated Parmesan cheese, divided
- 2 large tomatoes, thinly sliced
- ¼ cup balsamic vinegar, divided
- 1 pound cooked, cleaned shrimp, coarsely chopped
- 1 can (14 ounces) artichoke hearts, drained and coarsely chopped
- 1 bag (6 ounces) fresh baby spinach
- ¼ teaspoon salt
- ¼ teaspoon black pepper
- 1 cup shredded mozzarella cheese

SPECIAL AIDS
pastry brush

SERVES 6

COOKING TIME
10 MINUTES

Kitchen Tips

In this recipe, use cooked and cleaned shrimp from the freezer case or supermarket deli, or you can prepare the shrimp at home.

MAKING THE SHRIMP MELT

1. Preheat the broiler. Using your fingers, pull out some of the soft center from the bread to make a well for the toppings. Place bread cut-side up on a baking sheet. ▼

2. Broil bread until edges are golden brown, about 2 minutes.

3. In a large skillet, melt butter over medium heat; add garlic powder and cook for 1 minute. Using a pastry brush, brush butter onto cut-sides of bread, leaving some butter in pan; sprinkle 2 tablespoons Parmesan. Layer tomatoes on top; drizzle 1 tablespoon vinegar.

4. In the same skillet, cook shrimp, artichokes, spinach and 2 tablespoons vinegar over high heat, stirring, until spinach is wilted and mixture is heated through, about 4 minutes; add salt and pepper. Using a slotted spoon, transfer shrimp mixture to bread. ▼

5. Drizzle remaining vinegar over the shrimp mixture; sprinkle with remaining Parmesan and mozzarella.

6. Broil until cheeses are melted, about 3 minutes; transfer to a cutting board. Using a serrated knife, cut diagonally into individual servings. ▼

Attention to Detail

ABOUT MOZZARELLA

- This mild cheese is available in packaged and fresh varieties. Packaged mozzarella is factory produced and comes in low-fat and nonfat varieties. Because it melts so well, mozzarella is a favorite pizza ingredient and a good choice for cooking.

- Fresh mozzarella is moister and more delicately flavored than packaged mozzarella. It is usually made from whole milk and is often packed in water.

Shrimp & Pasta

This irresistible flavor combination is also perfect for pasta. Just sauté the toppings for these melts in a skillet; "then toss with cooked, drained pasta.

Mellow Vinegar

The balsamic vinegar called for in this recipe is darker and sweeter than other vinegars because it is aged in wooden casks.

Smoky Cheese

Jazz up these melts with the rich flavor of smoked mozzarella in place of the regular mozzarella. You'll find it in cheese shops and gourmet markets.

GOOD IDEA To enjoy these flavors at a picnic, just convert the melt to a sandwich. Use sliced fresh mozzarella cheese.

Variations

All-Star Veggie Melt

Make it veggie heaven with artichokes, sautéed sliced onions, red and yellow bell peppers and basil leaves.

Shrimp-Lovers' Pizza

For catch-of-the-day pizza, pile all the ingredients onto warmed prebaked pizza crusts and broil as directed.

Broccoli-Stuffed Pizza Rings

You Will Need

❧❧❧❧

FOR THE PIZZA RINGS

- 1 package (10 ounces) refrigerated pizza dough
- ½ cup plus 1 tablespoon coarsely grated Parmesan cheese, divided
- ⅓ cup shredded mozzarella cheese
- ¼ cup finely chopped broccoli, raw or cooked
- ¼ cup ricotta cheese
- 2 cloves garlic, minced (about 1 teaspoon)
- ¼ teaspoon crushed red pepper flakes
- ¼ teaspoon dried rosemary, crushed
- ¼ teaspoon salt
- ¾ cup prepared marinara sauce, at room temperature

SPECIAL AIDS

4 pieces aluminum foil, each 8 inches square

SERVES 4

COOKING TIME 20 MINUTES

Kitchen Tips

Using greased foil balls for the dough rings prevents the centers from closing as the rings bake.

ASSEMBLING THE PIZZA RINGS

1. Preheat oven to 425°F. Lightly grease a baking sheet. Divide pizza dough into 4 pieces. On a lightly floured surface, using your fingers, press each piece into a 10- x 3-inch rectangle. ▼

2. For the filling, in a small bowl, mix 5 tablespoons Parmesan, mozzarella, broccoli, ricotta, garlic, red pepper flakes, rosemary and salt.

3. Spoon one-quarter of filling onto the center of each dough strip, leaving a ¼-inch border around edges. Fold long sides of dough over filling; pinch edges firmly to seal. ▼

4. Bring ends of each filled dough strip together to form a ring; pinch firmly to seal. Transfer pizza rings to the prepared baking sheet.

5. Crumple each piece of foil into a small ball about 2 inches in diameter. Spray balls lightly with cooking spray and place a ball in the center of each pizza ring. ▼

BAKING & SERVING THE RINGS

1. Bake pizza rings until browned, about 20 minutes. Transfer to a wire rack; carefully remove foil balls from centers of pizza rings.

2. Place rings on individual plates; spoon about 3 tablespoons marinara sauce into center of each pizza ring. Sprinkle with remaining Parmesan; serve immediately.

Attention to Detail

CLASSIC PIZZA RINGS

Make these rings with a traditional Italian filling. Mix ½ cup mozzarella, ½ cup grated Romano, 2 tablespoons chopped olives, 2 cloves garlic, minced, ½ teaspoon oregano and pepper and salt to taste. Fill and bake as recipe directs.

Pizza Pizzazz

If your family includes fans of stuffed-crust pizza, they'll be sure to love these snacks: homemade filled pizza rings with a pool of tangy tomato sauce in the center.

Do-Ahead

Prepare these rings and chill for a day or freeze for up to one month. Put them into the oven right out of the fridge or freezer. Bake until browned.

Lighten Up

To keep these tasty snacks on the lighter side, use low-fat pizza crust and reduced-fat cheeses in the recipe.

GOOD IDEA Make this snack the center of a tasty meal. Serve it with a tossed salad and colorful spumoni ice cream for dessert.

Variations

Pizza Bagels

This is fast food with homemade appeal! Make simple open-faced pizza rings using bagels—brush with sauce and toppings for a quick snack or lunch.

Ham-and-Cheese Rings

Here's another filling for these tasty rings: Combine shredded Swiss cheese, diced ham and chopped sun-dried tomatoes. A honey-mustard sauce is a great dip!

Pizza-Stuffed Potatoes

You Will Need

FOR THE POTATOES

- **4   large baking potatoes**
- **2   teaspoons vegetable oil**
- **½   cup thinly sliced pepperoni, divided**
- **½   cup sour cream**
- **½   teaspoon salt**
- **¼   teaspoon freshly ground black pepper**
- **½   cup tomato sauce**
- **½   cup sliced mushrooms**
- **1   small green pepper, cut in thin strips (about ½ cup)**
- **½   cup shredded mozzarella cheese**
- **2   tablespoons grated Parmesan cheese**

SERVES 4

**BAKING TIME
1 HOUR**

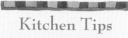

Kitchen Tips

- Choose mature baking potatoes, such as Idaho, for the best flavor and texture.

- Don't sacrifice flavor by using a microwave to bake a potato. While it certainly speeds cooking time, using the microwave fills the potato with steam, giving it a dense, heavy texture.

PREPARING THE POTATOES

1. Preheat oven to 450°F. Scrub the potatoes; pierce with a fork and rub with vegetable oil. Place potatoes on a baking sheet and bake until fork tender, about 45 minutes.

2. Halve potatoes lengthwise and scoop out flesh, leaving a ¼-inch-thick shell with skin. Set flesh aside. ▼

3. Chop ¼ cup sliced pepperoni. Cut remaining slices in half; set aside.

4. In a large bowl, mash together the potato flesh, sour cream, salt and pepper; add chopped pepperoni.

5. Spoon potato mixture back into shells and arrange on baking sheet. ▼

6. Top potatoes with tomato sauce, mushrooms, green pepper strips, remaining pepperoni, mozzarella and Parmesan. Bake until heated through, about 15 minutes. ▼

Attention to Detail

Just as on a traditional pizza, you can vary the toppings on these stuffed potatoes for a whole new taste sensation. Try one of the following combinations:

TACO PIZZA: Browned ground beef, taco seasoning mix, salsa, diced green chilies, shredded Monterey Jack cheese

POLYNESIAN PIZZA: Pineapple chunks, ham or prosciutto, coconut

VEGGIE PIZZA: Chopped roasted red peppers, eggplant, zucchini and tomatoes, grated Parmesan cheese

GOURMET PIZZA: Arugula, sliced artichoke hearts, sliced portabella mushrooms, sliced fontina cheese

GREEK PIZZA: Mini-shrimp, sliced Greek olives, crushed rosemary, crumbled feta cheese

PESTO PIZZA: Pesto, chopped fresh garlic, crumbled chèvre cheese

The Best Part

Twice-baked potatoes are doubly delicious. You can flavor the flesh with tasty herbs and spices to create a different filling. Plus, the twice-baked skin is much crisper.

Good for You

Potatoes have great health benefits; they are high in minerals, vitamins and protein.

Steam Busters

For crustier skins, pierce potatoes in a few places to allow steam to escape. Bake on a bed of rock salt on the baking sheet to absorb steam and crisp the skins.

■ **GOOD IDEA** These baked potatoes become the main event of a light meal when simply garnished or served with salad.

Variations

Some Like it Green

Use pesto in place of tomato sauce for a colorful twist. Try it with chicken instead of pepperoni and use red peppers instead of green.

Hash Brown Pizza

For a different slice of pizza, start with shredded potatoes cooked in a skillet; add pizza toppings. Cut your "pie" into wedges before serving.

Portobello Pizzas

You Will Need

FOR THE PIZZAS

- **4** large portobello mushroom caps
- **2** tablespoons olive oil
- **¼** teaspoon dried thyme
- **¼** teaspoon salt
- **½** pound hot Italian sausage, casings removed
- **3** tablespoons chopped plum tomatoes, seeds and juice removed
- **1** cup shredded mozzarella cheese
- **½** cup grated Parmesan cheese
- **2** tablespoons chopped fresh parsley (optional)

SPECIAL AIDS

pastry brush

SERVES 4

COOKING TIME
25-30 MINUTES

Kitchen Tips

- To prepare portobello mushroom caps, move the stems gently side to side until they break off. You can trim and clean the mushroom stems and use them to flavor vegetable or beef stock.

- When you are shopping for mushroom caps, choose ones that are firm, unbroken and evenly colored.

MAKING THE PORTOBELLO PIZZAS

1. Preheat oven to 400°F. Using a damp paper towel, wipe mushroom caps clean. Using a pastry brush, brush both sides of each mushroom with olive oil; sprinkle with thyme and salt. ▼

2. Place mushrooms stem-side down on a baking sheet. ▼

3. Bake mushrooms until completely softened, about 25 minutes. (Check mushrooms halfway through cooking time, covering the pan lightly with foil if mushrooms appear dry.)

4. Meanwhile, in a medium skillet, cook sausage over medium heat, breaking up with a spoon, until no longer pink, about 5 minutes; drain off excess oil.

5. Increase oven to broil. With a metal spatula, turn mushrooms over so they are stem-side up. ▼

6. Sprinkle equal amounts of sausage, tomato, mozzarella and Parmesan onto each mushroom; broil mushroom pizzas until cheese is browned and bubbly, about 3 minutes. Sprinkle pizzas with parsley, if desired; serve immediately.

Attention to Detail

VERSATILE PORTOBELLOS

The flavor of portobello mushrooms complements vegetable, meat and pasta dishes and can enhance almost any meal. Here is a sampling of the many uses for portobellos:

- Grill and slice mushrooms, then toss them on top of a green salad.
- Fill cooked mushrooms with scrambled eggs and sprinkle with chopped roasted red peppers for an unusual brunch dish.
- Mix chopped sautéed portobellos into wild rice or risotto.
- Add finely chopped portobellos to your favorite stuffing recipe.
- Layer cooked mushrooms in lasagna.

Terrific Tops

Like all pizzas, these snacks can be custom-made with any of your favorite ingredients, such as sliced olives, mozzarella, chopped basil, broccoli or sun-dried tomatoes.

Quick Dinner

Using pepperoni slices makes this recipe even easier to prepare. Cut the slices into small pieces and use them instead of sausage.

Go Light

It's easy to make low-calorie pizzas. Just substitute turkey sausage for Italian and top with low-fat mozzarella cheese.

GOOD IDEA Bowl guests over by using a portobello mushroom cap as a serving "dish" for marinated mushrooms.

Variations

Party Portobellos

Need a new hors d'oeuvre idea? Cut pizzas into wedges, then arrange them on a colorful plate or tray.

Made for a Bun

Grilled portobellos are a perfect size and texture to serve on a bun. Add lettuce, tomato, cheese and pickles.

Veggie & Pasta Oven Omelet

You Will Need

FOR THE OMELET

- 2 tablespoons vegetable oil
- ½ medium eggplant, peeled and cubed (about 2 cups)
- 1 large onion, chopped (about 1 cup)
- 1 large red or green bell pepper, chopped (about 1 cup)
- 1 cup frozen peas
- 1 package (3 ounces) cream cheese, cut into pieces
- ⅓ cup prepared pesto
- 6 large eggs
- ¾ cup milk
- ½ cup grated Parmesan cheese
- ½ teaspoon salt
- 4 cups cooked pasta, such as spaghetti

fresh basil leaves

SPECIAL AIDS

2-quart casserole dish

SERVES 6

**BAKING TIME
40 MINUTES**

Kitchen Tips

If you don't have leftover pasta, just cook 8 ounces of spaghetti or another favorite pasta for use in this recipe.

MAKING THE OMELET

1. Preheat oven to 375°F. In a large skillet, heat oil over medium heat. Add eggplant, onion and bell pepper; cook until onion is soft, about 10 minutes. Remove skillet from heat. Add peas, cream cheese and pesto; stir until cream cheese is melted. ▼

2. In a large bowl, whisk eggs, milk, Parmesan and salt. Stir in vegetable mixture and pasta until well combined; spoon into a 2-quart casserole dish. ▼

3. Bake omelet until edges are browned and center is set, about 40 minutes.

4. Let omelet stand for 5 minutes; cut into 6 even pieces. Transfer each piece to an individual serving plate; garnish with fresh basil. ▼

Attention to Detail

This recipe can be modified to suit your tastes and the ingredients you have on hand. Try any one of these combinations, or create your own:

OMELET VARIATIONS

SEASHORE OMELET: Use small shell pasta and add chopped cooked shrimp. Season with lots of fresh dill instead of the pesto.

"SAY CHEESE" OMELET: Replace the Parmesan in this recipe with 1 cup Monterey Jack or mozzarella.

ITALIAN OMELET: Sauté sweet Italian sausage in the skillet along with the vegetables.

GARDEN OMELET: Sauté fresh chopped tomatoes and zucchini with the onion.

Breakfast Bake

This savory breakfast recipe is a great way to use pasta left over from dinner the night before. A hearty dish, it's sure to please your hungry breakfast gang.

One-Pan Meal

Simplify the cleanup! Sauté the vegetables in a large ovenproof skillet. Then, mix the remaining ingredients; gently fold them into the skillet and bake as the recipe directs.

Eggwich!

Place a serving on an English muffin and top with sausage or bacon like a popular fast-food breakfast sandwich.

■ **GOOD IDEA** Who says you can't enjoy an omelet anytime? Paired with a fresh tossed salad, this dish makes a delightful dinner.

Variations

Speedy Salad

Leftover pasta makes a quick pasta salad. Toss with a jar of artichokes, along with their marinade, and cubes of salami, cheese or chicken.

Cheesy Casserole

Here's a novel twist on the classic macaroni and cheese: Use elbow macaroni instead of spaghetti in this recipe and add cubes of American cheese.

Colorful Coleslaw

You Will Need

FOR THE COLESLAW

- ½ medium head green cabbage
- ½ medium head red cabbage
- 1 medium apple, cored and diced (about 1 cup)
- 2 large carrots, grated (about 1 cup)
- 1 large green bell pepper, finely chopped (about 1 cup)
- 1 teaspoon celery seed

FOR THE DRESSING

- 1 can (12 ounces) evaporated skim milk
- 6 tablespoons cider vinegar
- ¼ cup light mayonnaise
- ¼ cup sugar
- ½ teaspoon salt

FOR THE GARNISH

- ¾ cup pecans, toasted and coarsely chopped

SERVES 12

PREPARATION TIME 20 MINUTES

Kitchen Tips

To preserve the vitamin C in cabbage, keep the heads whole until ready to use.

MAKING THE COLESLAW

1. Remove outer leaves from each head of cabbage; set aside. Cut cabbages into small wedges; remove cores. ▼

2. In a food processor fitted with the shredding disk, process cabbage wedges until shredded. ▼

3. In a large bowl, combine shredded cabbage, apple, carrot, bell pepper and celery seed, tossing to combine; set aside.

MAKING THE DRESSING

1. In a small bowl, combine milk and vinegar; let stand until thickened, about 30 seconds. Whisk mayonnaise, sugar and salt into vinegar mixture.

2. Pour dressing over coleslaw, stirring well to combine.

SERVING THE COLESLAW

1. Cut the tough stem end from each reserved cabbage leaf. Line a large glass bowl with leaves, alternating red and green leaves. ▼

2. Spoon the coleslaw onto the cabbage leaves. Sprinkle pecans over coleslaw; serve immediately.

Attention to Detail

ALL ABOUT CABBAGE

A staple ingredient around the world, cabbage comes in nearly 400 colorful varieties. Try a new one today!

- **GREEN CABBAGE** has smooth-textured light-green leaves and is delicious cooked and raw.
- **RED CABBAGE** leaves are purple or reddish-purple. They are tougher than green leaves, but a quick soak in a vinaigrette will tenderize them.
- **SAVOY CABBAGE** has frilly dark outer leaves that are often rolled around a meat stuffing.

Creative Salad

Customize this recipe with your favorite ingredients—toss in some thinly sliced red onion, sliced radishes, chopped pear, raisins or walnuts. Season the salad with mint, dill, parsley, gingerroot or rosemary.

Chef's Slaw

Make it a meal! Top this salad with thick strips of turkey, ham and Swiss cheese and a sliced or crumbled hard-boiled egg.

Kale Bowl

For naturally beautiful bowls, use decorative purple kale or crinkly savoy cabbage.

GOOD IDEA This is a "super bowl" for a football party. Serve with a platter of deli cold cuts and dark pumpernickel bread.

Variations

Bucket o' Slaw

A plastic sand pail makes a very cute container for a summer picnic. The kids can have fun with the pail when the yummy slaw has been eaten.

A Side of Salad

Line small bowls with cabbage leaves for pretty, individual servings. The leaves make a lovely dish for red potato salad, too.

Italian Bread Salad

You Will Need

FOR THE DRESSING

12	large fresh basil leaves
½	cup vegetable or olive oil
3	tablespoons red-wine vinegar
2	tablespoons water
1	packet (0.7 ounces) Italian dressing mix

FOR THE SALAD

2	large tomatoes
1	large cucumber
6	cups ¾-inch cubes day-old Italian bread
1	small red onion, finely chopped
1	yellow or red bell pepper, chopped

SERVES 8

PREPARATION TIME
30 MINUTES

Kitchen Tips

• After it's chopped, the basil should measure about ¼ cup, loosely packed.

• The texture of the bread cubes will change depending on when you serve the salad. For a crunchy salad, serve it immediately. If you prefer a softer salad, chill it for up to 4 hours before serving.

MAKING THE DRESSING

1. Stack basil leaves and fold lengthwise; using a sharp knife, cut crosswise into thin strips. Transfer strips to a small jar with a tight-fitting lid. ▼

2. Add oil, vinegar, water and dressing mix to the jar; secure the lid and shake well to thoroughly combine.

MAKING THE SALAD

1. Cut tomatoes in half horizontally. Gently squeeze tomatoes and shake to remove seeds. ▼

2. Using a large sharp knife, coarsely chop tomatoes. Slice cucumber lengthwise into quarters; cut quarters crosswise into ½-inch pieces.

3. In a large salad bowl, drizzle salad dressing over bread. ▼

4. Using salad tongs, toss bread to coat completely with dressing.

5. Add tomatoes, cucumber, red onion and bell pepper to the bread mixture, tossing to combine; serve immediately.

Attention to Detail

Day-old bread is ideal for this salad, but you can dry freshly baked bread to create the same crunchy texture.

OVEN-DRYING BREAD

1. Preheat oven to 350°F. Using a large sharp knife, cut a crusty loaf of Italian bread into medium-size cubes.

2. Spread bread cubes, in an even layer, on an ungreased baking sheet.

3. Bake bread cubes until dry, but not browned, 5-10 minutes.

Salad Days

This Italian salad, also known as *panzanella*, is a terrific use of your garden harvest. Vary the recipe by adding yellow pear tomatoes, cherry tomatoes or thin slices of celery.

Easy Option

Prepared bread cubes or croutons may be used instead of Italian bread in this dish. Let the salad stand before serving, so the bread will soften a little.

With Shrimp

Turn this salad into a magnificent lunch or dinner by topping it with some steamed or grilled shrimp.

GOOD IDEA To take this tasty salad to a picnic, prepare the vegetables and dressing, then toss in bread cubes just before serving.

Variations

Middle Eastern Salad

Here's another version: Replace the bread, vinegar and basil in this recipe with toasted pita wedges, lemon juice and fresh mint.

Mini Bread Salad Bowls

Present the salad in individual bread bowls. Just hollow out kaiser rolls and bake until lightly toasted, then fill with vegetable salad.

Tangy Beet Salad

You Will Need

❧❧❧❧❧

FOR THE DRESSING

- 2 tablespoons balsamic vinegar
- 1 tablespoon honey
- 2 teaspoons orange juice
- 1/2 teaspoon Dijon-style mustard
- 1/4 teaspoon peeled, grated gingerroot
- 1/4 teaspoon horseradish
- 1/4 teaspoon freshly ground black pepper
- 1/8 teaspoon salt
- 1/3 cup olive oil

FOR THE SALAD

- 8 large red-leaf lettuce leaves
- 3 medium carrots, peeled and cooked until tender
- 2 cans (9 ounces each) sliced beets, drained
- 1 medium orange
- 1/4 red onion, thinly sliced (about 2 tablespoons)
- 2 hard-boiled eggs, peeled and chopped
- 1/4 cup chopped pecans, toasted

SPECIAL AIDS

citrus stripper or vegetable peeler

SERVES 4

**PREPARATION TIME
30 MINUTES**

MAKING THE DRESSING

1. In a small bowl, whisk together vinegar, honey, orange juice, mustard, gingerroot, horseradish, pepper and salt.

2. Add oil in a slow, steady stream, whisking constantly, until dressing is well combined and slightly thickened; set aside.

MAKING THE SALAD

1. Line a large salad bowl with lettuce leaves; set aside. Using a sharp knife, cut carrots into 1/8-inch julienne strips; transfer to a large bowl. Cut beets into 1/4-inch-thick strips; add to carrots. ▼

2. Using a citrus stripper or a vegetable peeler, remove zest from orange in thin strips; add to beet mixture. ▼

3. Add onion to beet mixture; drizzle with dressing. Using 2 wooden spoons, toss salad thoroughly. Transfer salad to the lettuce-lined bowl.

4. Sprinkle hard-boiled eggs and pecans over salad; serve immediately. ▼

Attention to Detail

Roasted beets are an extraordinarily flavorful, colorful side dish—and a great alternative to potatoes!

ROASTED BEETS

1. Preheat oven to 350°F. Place fresh beets, greens removed, in a roasting pan.

2. Cover pan with foil; roast beets until fork-tender, about 1 hour.

3. Remove stem ends and skins; slice beets into 1/4-inch-thick slices.

4. Drizzle beet slices with olive oil or melted butter; add salt and pepper to taste. Serve immediately.

Beet Beauty

Shredded beets are a colorful way to perk up a green salad. They also lend a pretty pink color and zesty flavor to ordinary coleslaw.

Great Greens

If you buy fresh beets or grow them in your garden, don't discard the flavorful greens. Sauté them in butter; add a tablespoon of vinegar, a teaspoon of horseradish and salt and pepper to taste.

Creative Cuts

To jazz up this salad, cut beet slices into fun shapes using aspic cutters, then use them to garnish the salad.

■ GOOD IDEA

Host a Scandinavian smorgasbord with Swedish meatballs, cold cuts, herring and potato and beet salads.

Variations

Slivered Salad

For a quick summer salad, shred uncooked beets, carrots and cucumbers; toss with light dressing and sprinkle with chopped pecans.

Artful Option

Create a stunning composition of beet and carrot matchsticks fanned over lettuce leaves. Garnish the salad with sliced red onion and chopped egg.

Three Bean Salad

You Will Need

❦❦❦❦

FOR THE VINAIGRETTE

⅓ cup red-wine vinegar

2 tablespoons Dijon-style mustard

2 tablespoons lemon juice

¼ teaspoon salt

¼ teaspoon freshly ground black pepper

1 tablespoon chopped fresh rosemary or 1 teaspoon dried rosemary

⅔ cup olive oil

MAKES ABOUT 1 CUP

FOR THE SALAD

1 small zucchini

½ cup firmly packed chopped cilantro leaves, divided

1 small red onion, chopped (about ½ cup)

1 can (16 ounces) black beans, drained

1 can (16 ounces) dark red kidney beans, drained

1 can (16 ounces) pinto or white kidney beans, drained

1 cup frozen corn kernels, thawed

1 teaspoon minced garlic

½ teaspoon crushed red pepper flakes (optional)

SERVES 8

**PREPARATION TIME
20 MINUTES plus chilling**

MAKING THE VINAIGRETTE

1. In a medium bowl, using a whisk, combine red-wine vinegar, mustard, lemon juice, salt and pepper; mix well. Add rosemary; whisk until blended.

2. Add olive oil in a slow, steady stream, whisking constantly. Cover and refrigerate.

MAKING THE SALAD

1. Using a sharp knife, slice zucchini lengthwise into quarters; cut into ¼-inch-thick slices. ▼

2. Set aside 1 tablespoon cilantro leaves for garnish.

3. In a large bowl, combine zucchini, onion, black beans, red kidney beans, pinto beans, corn, garlic and remaining cilantro leaves. Add red pepper flakes, if desired. Stir in salad dressing, tossing to coat. ▼

4. Cover bowl; chill salad to blend flavors, about 30 minutes. Toss again before serving; garnish with reserved cilantro leaves.

Attention to Detail

There are a multitude of beans that you can use in this salad. Be creative; choose beans for their different colors and shapes to create a festive dish that looks as good as it tastes. Here are just a few suggestions:

• Black-eyed peas are named for the black dot on their beige skin; they have a strong vegetable-like flavor

• Cream-colored chickpeas have a mild, nutty flavor

• Lentils come in many colors, including green, red, yellow and black—each with its own flavor and texture

• Look for pretty, mottled beans, such as pintos and Christmas limas, with their interesting, two-tone skin

Did You Know?

Beans fall under the category of legumes. There are nearly 12,000 varieties of legumes — they are grown in every country in the world!

Heart Smart

Beans are a "heart healthy" food that contains vitamins, minerals, fiber and carbohydrates. They are high in protein and relatively low in calories.

Make it Hot

For an extra zing, try adding a tablespoon of chopped jalapeño peppers to this salad.

GOOD IDEA This colorful salad makes an easy meal idea. Serve to a houseful of weekend guests with warm corn bread.

Variations

Bean Burrito

For a quick lunchtime meal, wrap this tasty bean salad in a warm flour tortilla.

All Dressed Up

Offer a bottle of the red-wine vinaigrette as a gift. Attach the vinaigrette recipe to the bottle with a ribbon.

Easy Vegetable Garnishes

You Will Need

A variety of vegetables can be used to create different types of garnishes. Some choices are listed below:

FOR VEGETABLE FLOWERS

baby beets

bell peppers

carrots

mushrooms

red or white pearl onions

red, black or white radishes

zucchini

FOR VEGETABLE CHAINS

small bell or banana peppers

cucumbers

summer squash

zucchini

FOR VEGETABLE LEAVES

green bell peppers

brussels sprouts

herb sprigs

green onion tops

snow peas

FOR VEGETABLE CUPS OR BOWLS

bell peppers

small cucumbers

baby eggplant

gourds or mini pumpkins

baby pattypan squash

baby zucchini

RADISH MUSHROOMS
With a knife, make 4 cuts from the root end halfway up radish to make a stem. Slice crosswise just to the stem; remove scraps. Sprinkle "caps" with paprika.

VEGETABLE CHAINS
Cut cucumber and summer squash into ⅛-inch-thick slices. With a round cutter or knife, remove centers to form rings. Cut a slit in each ring and link together.

ONION FLOWERS
Make lengthwise cuts through tops of green onions; trim root ends to ½ inch from cuts. Score pearl onions to ½ inch from bases. Crisp 2 hours in ice water.

CARROT POSIES
Using a channeling tool, cut lengthwise ridges in peeled carrot. Slice crosswise and crisp in ice water. Press peppercorns onto centers; add snow peas for leaves.

BABY VEGGIE BOWLS
With an aspic cutter or knife, remove center from eggplant, baby squash or zucchini to form a bowl. Blanch and chill. Fill with dressing, cheese or dip.

OLIVE BEES
Cut a slit in each side of a pitted olive; press ends together gently. Push the tip of a carrot triangle into each side of the slit and into the large end opening.

A creative vegetable garnish can turn the simplest dish into a work of art

Colorful vegetables are natural accents for salads, individual plates, platters and party presentations. With a little imagination and the right tools, you can easily transform ordinary vegetables into standout garnishes.

Almost any vegetable can be carved, curled, snipped, stuffed or colored to create a garnish. Many vegetables have a delightful tendency to curl when thinly sliced and chilled in ice water; most will take on color from food coloring in their crisping liquid. Start with these techniques and whatever vegetables you have on hand and you'll never settle for a sprig of parsley again!

Finishing Touches

EASIER CUTTING
To make round vegetables easier to cut, create a stable surface by slicing off the bottom; this makes it much easier to hold on to the item as you work with it.

COLORING GARNISHES
Add food coloring to water used to store or curl vegetables. The vegetables will absorb the tints, giving your garnishes interesting color and variety.

For Best Results

• Most garnishes can be made with just a small sharp paring knife and a vegetable peeler, but items like a channeling tool and small aspic or cookie cutters add versatility to garnish making.

• If you must prepare a garnish ahead of time, cover it with damp paper towels and plastic wrap, then refrigerate.

Bell Pepper Flowers

Kitchen Tips

• Draining and rinsing canned
beans removes excess salt.

• To make nicely shaped petals,
choose uniform, short peppers.
If you find only long peppers,
make 2 smaller petals out of
each section.

PREPARING THE PEPPERS

1. Preheat oven to 350°F. Using a
small knife, cut bell peppers lengthwise
into quarters; remove stem, seeds and
membranes. ▼

2. Trim the narrow ends of pepper
pieces to a point to resemble flower petals;
set aside scraps. Transfer "petals," skin-
side down, to a baking sheet. Spoon
1 teaspoon cheese onto each petal. Bake
until cheese is melted, about 10 minutes.

ASSEMBLING THE FLOWERS

1. Transfer reserved pepper scraps to a
food processor; pulse until chopped, about
10 seconds. Transfer to a medium bowl.

2. In a fine mesh sieve, rinse and drain
black beans thoroughly. ▼

3. Add beans and salsa to chopped
pepper, stirring until well combined;
set aside ¼ cup salsa mixture.

4. Spoon remaining salsa mixture along
1 side of a serving platter to form "soil."
Slice green onion top in half lengthwise;
insert green onions into salsa mixture to
form "stems."

5. Alternately arrange 2 green, 2 red
and 2 yellow "petals" around each "stem"
to form a flower. ▼

6. Spoon half of reserved salsa mixture
into the center of each flower; top with
1 cherry tomato. Serve pepper flowers
with pita chips or tortilla chips.

Attention to Detail

Yellow and red bell peppers
can also be arranged to look
like springtime tulips:

PEPPER TULIPS

Cut peppers in half lengthwise;
core, stem and seed peppers. Trim
tops of peppers in a zigzag shape to
resemble a tulip. Fill peppers with
cheese and bake as directed. Add a
green onion stem before serving.

Peppy Pleaser

This colorful, beautiful snack will please the eye and the taste buds of Southwestern fans.

Holiday Fare

For appetizing color and flavor around the holidays, make these flower arrangements look like poinsettias! Use green and red bell peppers for petals and dot the centers with finely minced yellow bell peppers or capers.

Single-Serve

These peppers make stunning appetizers. Prepare one pepper posy for each person and serve on a pretty salad plate.

GOOD IDEA Make some "trees" along with these flowers. Stand broccoli florets in a block of herb-flavored cream cheese.

Variations

Chips and Dip

The salsa makes a tasty dip for tortilla chips. Add cilantro, minced onion and a squeeze of fresh lime juice to the salsa mixture.

Italian Flower Garden

Give these posies an Italian flavor: Top peppers with mozzarella and Parmesan, and use white beans instead of black in the salsa. Finish with basil leaves.

Stuffed Roasted Onions

You Will Need

FOR THE STUFFED ONIONS

- **6** large onions, such as Vidalia, Walla Walla, Spanish or sweet Bermuda
- **2** teaspoons olive oil, divided
- **½** pound spiced and cured link sausage, such as chorizo, linguiça, andouille or kielbasa
- **6** medium mushrooms, finely chopped (about ½ cup)
- **½** cup coarse fresh bread crumbs

SPECIAL AIDS

melon baller

SERVES 6

COOKING TIME
35-40 MINUTES

Kitchen Tips

- To store onions, cut the top off a pair of panty hose and drop the onions into a leg. Hang in a cool, dry place with good circulation for up to 2 months.

- The juices that are released when the onion flesh is torn or crushed are what cause the eyes to tear. The best way to minimize the "crying" is to use a very sharp knife. For a folk remedy, you can also try cutting the onions near a lit candle or a lit gas burner.

PREPARING THE ONIONS

1. Preheat oven to 375°F. Slice ½ inch from top of each onion, leaving a surface about 2 inches wide. Remove papery outer layers; leave root ends intact. ▼

2. Using a melon baller, scoop out the inside of each onion, leaving a shell that is 3 onion layers thick. ▼

3. Chop onion centers; set aside. Carefully trim off the root end of each onion to give it a flat base, but leave onion layers attached at the root end. ▼

MAKING THE STUFFING

1. Coat a baking dish with 1 teaspoon olive oil. Cut sausage into small cubes.

2. In a medium skillet, heat remaining olive oil over low heat; add sausage and cook, stirring, until lightly browned, about 5 minutes. Add 1¼ cups reserved chopped onions to pan; continue cooking over low heat until soft and translucent, about 7 minutes. Add mushrooms; cook 5 minutes longer. Remove pan from heat and add bread crumbs; mix well.

3. Spoon sausage mixture into onions, filling generously. Place stuffed onions in prepared baking dish. Bake until filling is browned and onion shell is slightly translucent but still firm, 35-40 minutes.

Attention to Detail

These onions work best in this recipe:

VIDALIA: Sweet, juicy, pale yellow onion with thick layers; only available May and June.

WALLA WALLA: Juicy, large, round and golden onion; available from June to September.

SPANISH: Large, round, yellow onion with a mild flavor; available from August to May.

SWEET BERMUDA: Large yellow or white onion with flattened ends and a mild flavor; available from March to June.

Fresh Air

To freshen the air in your kitchen after cooking the onions, combine water with vinegar and cloves; boil several minutes.

Sausage Stats

The best sausages to use in this dish are the flavorful smoked varieties, like Polish kielbasa, garlicky chorizo or linguiça, or spicy andouille.

Veggie Variation

For vegetarians, fill onions with cooked white and wild rice, olives, mushrooms and caramelized onions. Sprinkle with herbs before roasting.

GOOD IDEA Try using this stuffing in other hollowed-out vegetables, such as winter squash or colorful bell peppers.

Variations

Skip the Stuffing

For a simple side dish or salad enhancer, roast whole onions in chicken broth with olive oil and spices, basting occasionally, for 1 hour.

Slice and Bake

Here's a twist on the recipe, using the same ingredients: Cut raw onions into thick slices, top with mounds of stuffing and bake as recipe directs.

Maple-Glazed Squash Rings

You Will Need

🌿🌿🌿🌿🌿

FOR THE SQUASH RINGS

- 3 medium acorn squash
- 2 tablespoons butter or margarine
- ¼ cup maple syrup

SERVES 4

BAKING TIME
30 MINUTES

Kitchen Tips

- Since these squash rings are baked in a shallow pan or dish, you can cook them on the bottom oven rack while your entrée bakes or roasts above—very convenient when you're cooking for a crowd!

- For easier slicing, pierce the rind several times with a fork and then microwave the squash on **HIGH** for 2 minutes; let squash stand for 3 minutes before cutting.

- You can use either pure maple syrup or maple-flavored syrup for this recipe. Pure maple syrup is less sweet than the artificially flavored variety, so you might wish to use a little more.

- Store pure maple syrup in the refrigerator after opening. It will keep for up to 1 year.

MAKING THE SQUASH RINGS

1. Place squash on their sides on a cutting board. Using a large knife, trim off the ends and discard. Slice each squash into 4 rings about ¾ inch thick.

2. Using a small sharp knife, remove seeds and fibers from inside each ring by neatly cutting away a very thin layer of squash flesh. ▼

3. Preheat oven to 400°F. Place butter in a large baking pan. Place the pan in the oven until butter is melted, about 2 minutes. Remove from the oven; using a measuring spoon, transfer 1 tablespoon melted butter to a small bowl.

4. Spread remaining butter evenly in the bottom of the pan. Arrange squash rings in a single layer in the pan, fitting their points and grooves together. ▼

5. Drizzle rings with maple syrup and remaining melted butter, spreading with the back of a spoon to completely cover tops of squash. Bake for 20 minutes.

6. Remove the pan from the oven; using a spatula, carefully turn each squash ring over. Reduce oven heat to 350°F; return the pan to the oven and bake squash rings until they are easily pierced with the point of a knife, about 10 minutes longer.

Attention to Detail

WINTER SQUASH VARIETIES

Here are descriptions of several squash varieties, including their color, shape, flesh characteristics and how they're best cooked. Any one would work well in this recipe.

ACORN: dark green (turns to orange when ripened); sharp ridges and grooves; firm. Bake.	**BUTTERNUT:** cream-colored; gourd-shaped; orange; soft when cooked. Steam or boil.
BUTTERCUP: dark green; unevenly round, with small ringed depression in base; bright orange; soft when cooked. Bake unpeeled.	**HUBBARD:** pale blue-green; bumpy; large, with tapered ends; firm; holds shape well. Cut into individual serving pieces or dice and bake.

Maple Magic

Maple syrup lends foods a distinctive flavor. It's especially delicious with squash, nuts, apples, pork and other mild-flavored foods; its subtle character is easily overwhelmed by piquant or strong-flavored foods, such as beef, lamb, bell peppers or onions.

Squash Swap

This sweet maple glaze is a delicious complement for any winter squash. For a change, cut rings or wedges from a butternut, Hubbard or turban squash and proceed as directed.

■ **GOOD IDEA**
To make these rings extra special, fill the center holes with prepared stuffing or wild rice pilaf.

Variations

Glazed Carrots

Why not use a maple glaze on other recipes? For another special side dish, heat ¼ cup maple syrup with 1 tablespoon butter; toss cooked carrots in the glaze.

Crumb Topping

Give squash rings a tasty coating. Mix bread crumbs with melted butter and brown sugar; top the rings with the mixture and bake on a buttered baking sheet.

Stuffed Zucchini Boats

PREPARING THE ZUCCHINI BOATS

1. Fill a medium saucepan two-thirds full with water; bring to a boil over high heat. Meanwhile, trim the ends from the zucchini; set aside. Using a crinkle vegetable cutter, cut the zucchini into 3-inch-long pieces; cut each piece in half lengthwise. ▼

2. Using a melon baller or a small teaspoon, scoop out centers of each zucchini slice, leaving a ¼-inch border on all sides; set aside centers. ▼

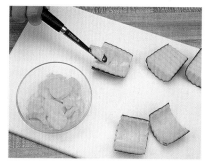

3. Fill a medium bowl with cold water. Line a large plate with paper towels. Place zucchini boats in boiling water. Cover; boil for 2 minutes. Transfer boats to cold water; place, cut-side down, on the prepared plate to drain.

4. Put reserved zucchini ends and centers into boiling water. Boil ends and centers until softened, 5-7 minutes; drain and chop finely.

MAKING THE FILLING

1. Preheat oven to 350°F. In a large skillet, heat 2 tablespoons olive oil over low heat. Add onion and celery; sauté until tender, about 4 minutes. Add garlic; sauté about 1 minute longer.

2. Remove the skillet from heat; add bread crumbs, sausage, Parmesan, basil, parsley, pepper and chopped zucchini. Stir to blend, adding more oil if too dry.

STUFFING AND BAKING THE ZUCCHINI BOATS

1. Place a wire rack over a baking sheet. Using a small spoon, fill zucchini boats with crumb mixture, mounding mixture to a ½-inch height. Place filled boats, skin-side down, on the rack. ▼

2. Bake zucchini boats for 15 minutes. Increase oven temperature to broil. Broil zucchini boats, 5 inches from heat, until lightly browned, about 1 minute longer; serve immediately.

Waste Not

A little meat goes a long way in this hearty dish. Try using leftover turkey, steak, chicken or pork roast in place of the sausage. A can of cooked shrimp is also a great substitute.

Keep it Cool

In the summertime, allow this filling to cool completely, then stuff the zucchini boats and serve immediately.

Garden Garnish

If you're using zucchini from your garden in this recipe, harvest a couple of the pretty yellow blossoms as a colorful garnish for your serving platter.

GOOD IDEA Start a new tradition! For your next Thanksgiving meal, stuff butternut and acorn squash with this meaty stuffing.

Variations

Fancy Cups

For a different look, score the zucchini with a citrus stripper and cut it into tall slices. Scoop a small well from the top of each slice; fill and bake as directed.

Honey-Ham Boats

Chopped honey-baked ham mixed with a teaspoon of Dijon-style mustard lends delicious flavor to these boats. Just use it in place of the cooked sausage.

Tasty Vegetable Bundles

You Will Need

❧❧❧❧

FOR THE MUSHROOM FILLING

- 6 ounces whole mushrooms
- 2 large stalks celery
- 1 medium onion
- 2 tablespoons butter or margarine
- 1 medium clove garlic, crushed
- 1 tablespoon balsamic vinegar
- ½ teaspoon dried thyme
- ½ teaspoon salt
- ⅛ teaspoon black pepper

FOR THE RED PEPPER FILLING

- 1 jar (7 ounces) roasted red peppers, drained
- 1 medium onion
- 1 tablespoon olive oil
- ¼ cup pitted, finely chopped kalamata olives
- ½ teaspoon dried basil
- ¼ teaspoon salt
- ⅛ teaspoon black pepper
- ¼ cup crumbled feta cheese

FOR THE BUNDLES

- ½ cup (1 stick) butter or margarine, melted
- 32 sheets (17- x 12-inch) phyllo dough, thawed
- 16 green onion tops

MAKES 16 BUNDLES

**BAKING TIME
15 MINUTES**

MAKING THE MUSHROOM FILLING

1. Finely chop mushrooms, celery and onion. In a large skillet, melt butter over medium-high heat. Add mushrooms, celery, onion and garlic; cook, stirring constantly, until mushrooms are cooked through and the liquid has evaporated, about 10 minutes. Stir in the balsamic vinegar, thyme, salt and pepper; cook 1 minute longer. Transfer the mixture to a small bowl; let cool.

MAKING THE RED PEPPER FILLING

1. Finely chop peppers and onion. In a large skillet, heat oil over medium heat. Add onion; sauté until softened, 5-7 minutes. Stir in peppers, olives, basil, salt and pepper; cook until the mixture is heated through, about 3 minutes longer. Remove skillet from heat; stir in feta. Transfer mixture to a small bowl; let cool.

MAKING THE BUNDLES

1. Preheat oven to 350°F. Grease a baking sheet. Cut 2 sheets of phyllo in half crosswise, keeping the remaining sheets of phyllo dough covered with plastic wrap. ▼

2. Layer cut pieces of phyllo, brushing melted butter between layers; brush top of phyllo stack with melted butter. ▼

3. Spoon 2 tablespoons of mushroom filling into the center of the stacked phyllo. Bring the corners of the phyllo together just above the filling; twist to close. Transfer the bundle to the prepared baking sheet. Repeat with remaining phyllo and both fillings. ▼

4. Tie a green onion top around the "neck" of each bundle. Lightly spray the bundles with vegetable cooking spray. Bake bundles until golden brown, about 15 minutes. Serve immediately.

Classic Bundles

These tasty bundles are fashioned after a classic appetizer called beggar's purses, made popular by New York's Quilted Giraffe restaurant. The original version contains caviar and a thick cream called crème fraîche.

Puff Preference

Try using puff pastry instead of the phyllo dough to make these appetizers.

Lunch Munch

Spread any leftover filling on a halved bagel and top with mozzarella cheese; broil for 2 minutes.

■ GOOD IDEA These bundles are usually served as appetizers, but they also make a truly special side dish for meat or poultry.

Variations

Spicy Filling

For a zesty snack, combine sautéed red onion and browned ground beef; season with chili powder, salt and pepper. Fill bundles as directed.

Sweet Package

For dessert bundles, fill the packets with apple pie filling. Bake as directed; tie the necks of the bundles with strips of fresh apple peel.

Corn Bread & Sausage Stuffing

You Will Need

ଈଈଈ

FOR THE STUFFING

½ pound sweet Italian sausage

1 teaspoon olive oil

1 medium onion, coarsely chopped (about ¾ cup)

1 large celery stalk, coarsely chopped (about ½ cup)

2 packages (7 ounces each) corn toaster pastries

1 tablespoon butter or margarine

1 cup coarsely chopped pecans

1 tart apple, such as Granny Smith, McIntosh or Gala, peeled and chopped

2 tablespoons lemon juice

1 teaspoon dried marjoram

½ teaspoon nutmeg

½ teaspoon salt

½ cup chicken broth

SERVES 6

BAKING TIME 45 MINUTES

Kitchen Tips

To substitute standard-size corn muffins for the pastries in this recipe, cut muffins in half and toast under a broiler until lightly browned.

MAKING THE STUFFING

1. Preheat oven to 350°F. Grease a 13- x 9-inch baking pan. Using a small knife, remove casings from sausage. ▼

2. Break sausage into small pieces. In a medium skillet, heat olive oil over medium-low heat. Add sausage; cook, stirring, until crumbly and no longer pink, about 5 minutes. Pour off all fat from skillet; discard. Add onion and celery to the skillet; cook 1 minute longer. Transfer sausage mixture to a large bowl.

3. Toast corn pastries; let cool. Break corn pastries into small pieces; add to sausage mixture. ▼

4. In a small skillet, melt butter over medium heat. Add pecans and sauté for 2 minutes, stirring constantly.

5. In a small bowl, combine apple and lemon juice. Add apple mixture to sausage mixture. Add sautéed pecans, marjoram, nutmeg and salt, tossing mixture to combine. Stir in broth until mixture is moistened. ▼

6. Transfer stuffing to the prepared baking pan. Cover pan with foil; bake for 30 minutes. Uncover stuffing; bake for 15 minutes longer.

Attention to Detail

THE RIGHT STUFFING

Vary your stuffing flavor. Substitute the following breads for all or part of the corn pastries in this recipe:

• **Whole-wheat or other whole grain bread for chicken or turkey**

• **Sourdough bread for Cornish game hens or winter squash**

• **Rye bread for pork**

• **Raisin bread for poultry or pork**

Sandwich Stuff

It's not just another turkey sandwich if it has a layer of leftover stuffing! Serve hot turkey and stuffing on a bun with gravy for a hearty lunch.

Stuffed Pork

Love this stuffing? Try filling a boneless pork tenderloin with it. Or cut pockets into pork chops and fill 'em up.

Enuff Stuff

This versatile recipe makes enough to stuff one 10-pound turkey, 12 pork chops, 6 acorn squash or 2 chickens. It can also be halved or doubled to suit any meal.

GOOD IDEA Play up this recipe's flavors. Adorn your table with multicolored Indian corn and red, green and yellow apples.

Variations

Stuffed Squash

Fill autumn with flavor! For a main dish, cut acorn squashes in half; scoop out the seeds and mound uncooked stuffing into centers before baking.

Casserole Dinner

Make a casserole starring this recipe. Cover turkey slices with uncooked stuffing and bake. Top individual servings with a tart cranberry compote.

Cashew Broccoli Au Gratin

You Will Need

FOR THE BROCCOLI AU GRATIN

2½	pounds fresh broccoli (about 2 large bunches)
¼	cup (½ stick) butter or margarine
¼	cup all-purpose flour
2	cups whole milk
1	cup grated sharp Cheddar cheese (about 4 ounces)
½	teaspoon ground nutmeg
¼	teaspoon salt
1	cup toasted whole cashews

SERVES 6

PREPARATION TIME
20 MINUTES

Kitchen Tips

• For best results, use broccoli with tightly closed dark green buds and crisp stems.

• Immediately rinsing cooked broccoli in cold water sets its color and flavor.

• A wire whisk is the best tool for blending sauce as it cooks. Whisk constantly, so it thickens without separating or becoming lumpy.

PREPARING THE BROCCOLI

1. Trim broccoli ends, leaving about 3 inches of stem. Using a sharp knife, cut broccoli into bite-size florets.

2. Cook broccoli in boiling water for 5 minutes; drain. Rinse broccoli in cold water and drain again.

MAKING THE SAUCE

1. In a small heavy skillet, melt butter over medium heat. Using a wire whisk, stir in flour; continue cooking, whisking constantly, until well blended and bubbly, about 3 minutes. ▼

2. Add milk, a little at a time, whisking constantly. Continue whisking over medium heat until sauce comes to a boil; immediately reduce heat to low and continue cooking until sauce is thick and smooth, about 3 minutes longer. Add Cheddar cheese; stir until melted. Remove the pan from heat; add nutmeg and salt.

ASSEMBLING THE BROCCOLI AU GRATIN

1. Preheat oven broiler. Lay broccoli florets in a shallow baking dish. Drizzle sauce over broccoli, leaving a 1-inch border uncovered. ▼

2. Arrange cashews in a ring on the uncovered area of the broccoli. ▼

3. Broil 4 inches from heat until cheese is lightly browned, 5-8 minutes. Serve.

Attention to Detail

TIPS FOR PERFECT CHEESE SAUCE

• Cook the butter very carefully; if it burns, it will make the sauce bitter.

• Don't use low-calorie cheeses; they don't melt as well as regular cheeses.

• Though not as flavorful as natural cheese, processed cheeses melt more easily. Try a little of both in your next cheese sauce.

Veggie Power

Not only is this a tasty dish, it also packs a very healthful punch! Did you know that broccoli is the number one veggie in overall nutritional content?

Ham it Up

Make it a main dish—place a layer of thinly sliced deli ham in the bottom of the dish before adding the broccoli and cheese.

Simple Switch

For a different dish, skip the sauce and sauté garlic in olive oil; add broccoli and cook until heated through. Sprinkle with Parmesan and serve.

GOOD IDEA If you don't have cashews, try a garnish of water chestnuts, French-fried onions or chow mein noodles.

Variations

Vegetable Medley

This wonderfully rich sauce will add new life to other favorite vegetables! Create a new combination with cauliflower, broccoli and carrots.

Use Your Noodle!

To turn this dish into a satisfying meal, layer hot cooked noodles in a buttered casserole dish; top with the broccoli and cheese sauce and bake as directed.

Bread Basics

You Will Need

BASIC ROLLS

1½ cups water

½ cup milk

2 tablespoons sugar, divided

1 package active dry yeast

¼ cup (½ stick) butter or margarine, melted

6½ cups all-purpose flour, divided

2 teaspoons salt

MAKES 2 DOZEN ROLLS

Technique Tips

• **Be sure to cover the dough ball with a damp cloth or plastic wrap and set to rise in a warm, draft-free place. It will double in size in about 1 hour.**

• **To make a soft brown crust, brush top of bread with melted butter or margarine before or after baking.**

• **For a crisp brown crust, brush top with a beaten egg during the last 10 minutes of baking.**

• **For a tasty topping, brush bread before baking with a beaten egg and sprinkle with kosher salt or your choice of seeds—caraway, poppy or sesame.**

• **Baked bread freezes well, provided it is cooled, wrapped in plastic food wrap, then aluminum foil. Thaw in the refrigerator overnight. Preheat oven to 375°F. and reheat bread 5-6 minutes before serving.**

HEATING INGREDIENTS
Combine water, milk and 1 tablespoon sugar over medium-high heat until the mixture reaches about 110°F. Check with an instant-read thermometer.

MIXING SOFT DOUGH
Add remaining sugar, butter, 3 cups flour and salt; beat until smooth. Use hands to mix in enough remaining flour, ½ cup at a time, to make a soft dough.

LETTING DOUGH RISE
Shape dough into a smooth ball, place in a large greased bowl and rotate the ball until outside surface is covered with grease. Cover; let rise until doubled.

ACTIVATING YEAST
Pour warm mixture into a large mixing bowl; sprinkle in yeast and stir until dissolved. Set aside until frothy, about 6 minutes.

KNEADING DOUGH
Turn dough out onto lightly floured board and knead by hand until smooth and elastic, about 8 minutes. Add small amounts of flour only if necessary.

SHAPING AND BAKING
Punch dough down and turn out onto lightly floured surface; let rest 5 minutes. Shape, let rise until doubled; bake at 400°F. until brown, 12-15 minutes.

What could be better than starting the day with homemade bread straight from the oven?

Basic yeast breads are really nothing more than a mixture of flour, sugar and water or milk with yeast to make the dough rise. The diversity of bread recipes is simply due to varying the ingredients and shaping the dough. Beautiful breads may look difficult to make at home, but it is easier than you might think. Just follow the steps shown here for successful breadmaking basics, and from there you can learn more complicated bread recipes and aspects of shaping dough. Reviving the tradition of homemade breads is a savory experience; there's nothing quite like the smell—or the taste—of oven-fresh bread.

Tools of the Trade

KNEADING SURFACE
A reliable oven and a large, flat work surface are key to bread baking. Wood or marble is perfect for kneading. Racks for rising and cooling are additional aids.

SHAPING DOUGH
Shape dough after the first (and before the second) rising. Punch it down and turn it out onto work surface. Here, rolls are made with small dough balls.

For Best Results

- **Bring ingredients to room temperature before you begin. Make bread in a draft-free room.**

- **Add just enough flour to keep dough from sticking to the work surface when you knead and shape it; too much will ruin its consistency.**

- **When making rolls, divide dough into equal parts.**

Classic Sourdough Bread

You Will Need

FOR THE BREAD

- **7 cups bread flour or all-purpose flour, divided**
- **2 cups warm water (105°F-110°F)**
- **1 cup sourdough starter**
- **1½ packages active dry yeast**
- **2 teaspoons salt**
- **2 teaspoons sugar**
- **2 tablespoons cornmeal**

SPECIAL AIDS

dough-hook attachment for an electric mixer

MAKES 2 LOAVES

**BAKING TIME
40 MINUTES plus rising**

Kitchen Tips

- **Flour has a tendency to settle in the bag. Sift it or stir it vigorously before measuring.**
- **Yeast is a living organism that will die in very hot water. The temperature of the water in this recipe should be similar to that of a baby's bath.**
- **If you maintain the starter weekly, it will keep indefinitely in the refrigerator.**

MAKING THE DOUGH

1. In a large bowl, using an electric mixer fitted with a dough hook and set on medium speed, combine 2 cups flour, water, sourdough starter, yeast, salt and sugar; beat for 2 minutes.

2. With the mixer on low, add 2 cups flour, a little at a time, until combined. Increase speed to high; beat until smooth and sticky, about 3 minutes longer. With the mixer on low, beat in an additional 2 cups flour, a little at a time.

3. Turn dough onto a lightly floured surface; knead in remaining flour, a little at a time, until dough is smooth and elastic, about 10 minutes. ▼

4. Oil a large bowl; transfer dough to the bowl, turning to coat. Cover the bowl with plastic wrap; set in a warm place and let dough rise until doubled in size, about 1 hour.

MAKING THE BREAD

1. Punch down dough; divide in half. Sprinkle cornmeal onto a large baking sheet. Shape each piece of dough into a smooth, tight ball. Transfer each ball of dough to the baking sheet; cover with a towel. Let dough rise until doubled in size, about 45 minutes.

2. Preheat oven to 400°F. With a sharp knife, make four ¼-inch-deep slashes in a crisscross pattern on each loaf. ▼

3. Bake bread until golden brown, about 40 minutes; transfer to a wire rack to cool completely.

Attention to Detail

Use these easy instructions to make classic homemade sourdough starter:

SOURDOUGH STARTER

1. In a large bowl, combine 1½ cups bread flour, ½ cup rye flour, ½ package active dry yeast and 2 cups bottled springwater. Cover the bowl with a cloth and let sit at room temperature for 3 days. The mixture will bubble, smell slightly sour, darken slightly and collect a watery liquid on top.

2. On the fourth day, stir in ½ cup flour and ½ cup water; repeat on the fifth day. Use starter in bread dough or refrigerate in a sealed container.

3. For longer storage, once a week remove 1 cup starter; replace with ½ cup flour and ½ cup water.

Great Start

Sourdough bread is made with a live yeast starter—a mixture of flour, water and yeast that has been allowed to ferment for at least a few days. For this recipe, you can make your own starter or purchase it through catalogs or bakeries.

Flavor-Filled

The slightly sour, tangy flavor of sourdough bread gives extra zing to sandwiches, makes magnificent croutons and is a tasty bowl for dips. But beware, you might find yourself eating every delicious slice all by itself.

■ **GOOD IDEA**
Cubes of this savory bread are perfect for dipping. Try it with a traditional Swiss fondue of Gruyère and white wine.

Variations

Sourdough Rolls
Take a break from dull dinner rolls—make flavorful sourdough rolls instead. Form the dough into 24 rounds and bake until golden brown, about 25 minutes.

Rye Sourdough
To make a super savory sourdough loaf, replace 1 1/2 cups of the bread flour with rye flour and knead in 1/4 cup caraway seeds. For variety, shape the loaves into ovals.

Cheddar-Green Onion Scones

You Will Need

❦❦❦❦❦

FOR THE SCONES

- 2 cups all-purpose flour
- 4 teaspoons baking powder
- 1 teaspoon salt
- 1 teaspoon sugar
- 5 tablespoons cold butter, cut into small pieces
- ¾ cup whipping cream
- 3 eggs, divided
- ½ cup shredded Cheddar cheese
- ¼ cup finely chopped green onions (about 5 green onions)
- 1 tablespoon water

SPECIAL AIDS

2-inch biscuit cutter
pastry brush

MAKES 12-14 SCONES

BAKING TIME
12-15 MINUTES

Kitchen Tips

- If you do not have a 2-inch biscuit cutter, you can use the top of a glass to cut the scones.

- To make these scones quickly, use a food processor. Pulse dry ingredients until combined. Add butter; pulse just until blended. Add cream, eggs, cheese and green onions; pulse again just until blended. Turn the dough onto a lightly floured surface; proceed as the recipe directs.

MAKING THE DOUGH

1. Preheat oven to 400°F. In a large bowl, combine flour, baking powder, salt and sugar. Using 2 knives or your fingers, cut in butter until thoroughly blended. ▼

2. In a medium bowl, whisk cream and 2 eggs until well blended. Stir in cheese and green onions. Add the cream mixture to the flour mixture; stir just until a sticky dough forms.

MAKING THE SCONES

1. Turn dough onto a lightly floured surface; knead, no more than 10 times. (The dough will be slightly sticky; it should stick to your fingers. If it is too sticky to work with, add more flour, a teaspoon at a time.) ▼

2. Press dough into a ¾-inch-thick rectangle. Using a 2-inch biscuit cutter, cut dough into rounds. Transfer rounds to an ungreased baking sheet. Gently combine dough scraps and press to a ¾-inch thickness for additional biscuits.

3. Beat remaining egg with water. Using a pastry brush, brush egg wash onto scones. ▼

4. Bake scones until golden brown, 12-15 minutes. Serve immediately or at room temperature.

Attention to Detail

CUTTING IN

To "cut in" an ingredient means to incorporate a cold fat, such as butter, with flour or a flour mixture until the combination forms small particles. You can perform this technique by using 2 knives, 2 forks, a pastry blender or your fingertips. A food processor fitted with a metal blade also works well, but be sure to pulse the food processor, keeping a close eye on the consistency of the dough.

Scone Story

It's said that this quick bread is named after the Stone (or scone) of Destiny, the place where Scottish kings were once crowned.

Save for Later

Make the scones when you have spare time, then freeze them in an airtight container for up to 1 month.

Walnut-Fig

For a different flavor, replace the Cheddar and green onions in this recipe with ½ cup chopped walnuts and ¾ cup chopped dried figs. Add more sugar, using 2 tablespoons altogether.

GOOD IDEA Scones may be expected at tea or a brunch, but mini savory scones make great surprise hors d'oeuvres as well.

Variations

Scone-wich

For a delicious, homemade alternative to English-muffin breakfast sandwiches, serve scrambled eggs and bacon on one of these scones.

Better Butter

Traditional scones may be slathered in sweet butter, but to bring out the full flavor of these scones, use an herb butter, such as one made with rosemary or thyme.

Glazed Bird Rolls

You Will Need

FOR THE ROLLS

- 1 package (16 ounces) frozen roll dough, thawed as package directs
- 1 egg
- 1 tablespoon water

FOR THE GLAZE

- 2 cups sifted confectioners' sugar
- ¼ cup hot water
- 1 teaspoon butter or margarine, melted

SPECIAL AIDS

wooden skewer

MAKES 10-12 ROLLS

BAKING TIME
15 MINUTES

Kitchen Tips

- Keep the work surface lightly floured while you shape the rolls to prevent the dough from sticking.
- Be sure to follow the directions for rising and oven temperature on your packaged dough. Some dough requires rising time after it has been shaped.

PREPARING FOR THE ROLLS

1. Follow dough package directions for preheating oven. Lightly grease 2 baking sheets. Whisk together egg and water.

SHAPING THE BIRD ROLLS

1. For each bun, break off a 2-inch round piece of dough. Shape round into bird's body; gently shape the tail. ▼

2. Break off another small piece of dough, slightly smaller than the first piece, to form the head. Shape beak and crest and bottom of neck.

3. Press a small indentation into body where head will be attached. Brush base of neck with some egg mixture and fit into indentation. ▼

4. Break off 2 smaller pieces of dough and shape each into a wing. Attach wings with some egg mixture. Press a wooden skewer deeply into head to form eyes. Repeat with remaining dough. ▼

BAKING THE ROLLS

1. Arrange rolls, 2 inches apart, on prepared baking sheets. (Check dough package for rising requirements.) Brush with remaining egg mixture. Bake until golden, about 15 minutes. Transfer baking sheets to wire racks to cool.

2. For the glaze, mix confectioners' sugar, hot water and butter together. Brush warm rolls with glaze.

Attention to Detail

To shape snail rolls, roll out dough and cut into 2-inch-wide strips. Brush three-fourths of each strip with a cinnamon, sugar and butter glaze, if desired. Roll dough from one end to form snail shell. Shape a small head at opposite end and form two small feelers on top of head.

Quick Change

Stir 1 teaspoon each dried parsley and minced onion into the dough for a tasty herb roll.

Festive Fun

For Easter, serve the rolls on a bed of green-tinted shredded coconut and surrounded with candy eggs or jelly beans.

Kid Stuff

Serve rolls at a kid's breakfast party along with animal-shaped French toast and pancake cutouts topped with whipped cream, cherries and chocolate morsels.

GOOD IDEA Attach name tags to bird rolls and use as place cards for special meals.

Variations

Animal Art

Instead of bird rolls, try making different kinds of animals. Some ideas include dogs, cats, snails or anything your imagination can create.

Fish Food

Dress up a simple midweek meal by serving fish-shaped rolls with a hearty seafood chowder. The entire family will love them.

Garlic Sage Knots

You Will Need

❦❦❦❦❦

FOR THE KNOTS

¼ cup (½ stick) butter or
    margarine, divided

8 shallots, finely chopped
    (about ⅔ cup)

3 medium cloves garlic,
    minced (about
    1½ teaspoons)

6½-7 cups all-purpose flour,
    divided

2 packages active dry yeast

1 tablespoon finely chopped
    fresh sage or 1 teaspoon
    dried sage, crushed

2 cups water

2 tablespoons sugar

½ teaspoon salt

MAKES 16 GARLIC KNOTS

**BAKING TIME
15-20 MINUTES**

Kitchen Tips

• **Rising and baking times will
be slightly shorter if all your
bread ingredients are at room
temperature.**

• **Rolls can be stored at room
temperature for up to 3 days.**

MAKING THE KNOTS

1. In a small skillet, melt 1 tablespoon butter over medium heat. Add shallots and garlic; sauté until soft, about 3 minutes. Set aside. In a large bowl, combine 2 cups flour, yeast and sage.

2. In a medium saucepan, combine remaining butter, water, sugar and salt; heat over low heat just until warm and butter is almost melted, or until the mixture registers 120°F-130°F on an instant-read thermometer. Add sautéed garlic and shallots and water mixture to flour mixture. Using an electric mixer set on low speed, beat for 30 seconds, scraping sides of bowl.

3. With the mixer on high speed, beat the dough for 3 minutes. Stir in all but ¼ cup of the remaining flour. Turn the dough onto a lightly floured surface. Knead 6-8 minutes, working in the remaining flour to make a soft dough that is smooth and elastic. ▼

4. Shape the dough into a ball; place in a lightly greased bowl, turning once to coat. Cover; let dough rise in a warm place until doubled in size, about 1 hour.

5. Punch down dough; turn dough onto a lightly floured surface. Cover; let stand 10 minutes.

6. Preheat oven to 375°F. Grease 2 baking sheets. Divide dough into 16 equal pieces. Roll each piece of dough into a 12-inch-long rope. ▼

7. Working with one rope of dough at a time, fold a rope in half and tie in a loose knot. Transfer the knots to the prepared baking sheets. ▼

8. Cover the knots with plastic wrap or a kitchen towel; let rise in a warm place until nearly doubled in size, about 30 minutes. Bake the knots until golden brown, 15-20 minutes. Transfer the knots to wire racks; serve warm.

Crispy Crust

To give the knots a crisp outer coating, brush the formed dough with a mixture of water and egg whites before baking.

Garlic Tips

When buying garlic, look for firm, plump bulbs, heavy for their size, with dry skins. Avoid garlic found in the refrigerated section of the grocery store; these bulbs might be soft.

Shape Up

Use this dough to make rolls in all sorts of shapes—try cloverleafs, "cigars" or simple puffs.

■ **GOOD IDEA** Serve garlic knots hot from the oven with a simple meal of spicy pasta and a fresh green salad.

Variations

Simple Sticks

For tasty breadsticks, let the dough rise, then divide it into 16 pieces. Roll into 10-inch ropes. Immediately brush with egg wash and bake 15-20 minutes.

Garlic Bread

For these classic loaves, slice baguettes in half; spread with butter and sprinkle with shallots and garlic. Wrap in foil; heat at 325°F for 15 minutes. Garnish with parsley.

Potato Bread

You Will Need

FOR THE POTATO BREAD

1	medium baking potato, peeled and coarsely chopped
1	cup milk
2	tablespoons (¼ stick) butter or margarine
2	tablespoons sugar
1	teaspoon salt
1	package active dry yeast
5-5½	cups all-purpose flour
1	egg white
2	teaspoons water
⅓	cup grated Parmesan cheese

MAKES 2 LOAVES

**BAKING TIME
35 MINUTES plus rising**

Kitchen Tips

- To test potato for doneness, insert the tines of a fork into the center of a potato piece; there should be no resistance.

- After cooking potatoes, drain immediately so they won't absorb excess water.

- Slashing these loaves before baking allows them to rise and expand without cracking along the sides or bottom.

MAKING THE DOUGH

1. Place potato in a medium saucepan; add water to cover. Boil over high heat until fork tender, 10-15 minutes. Drain, pouring ¾ cup liquid into a large bowl; set aside until warm (105°F-110°F).

2. In a medium bowl, combine potato, 2 tablespoons milk, butter, sugar and salt. Puree with an electric mixer on medium; beat in remaining milk. ▼

3. Sprinkle yeast over reserved liquid; let stand until foamy. Stir in potato mixture. Add 3 cups flour; with mixer on medium, beat until smooth and elastic. Stir in enough remaining flour to make a soft dough. Turn onto a floured surface; knead until smooth and small bubbles form, 8-10 minutes. ▼

4. Grease a large bowl. Transfer dough to the prepared bowl, turning to coat. Cover dough; let rise in a warm place until doubled in size, about 1 hour.

SHAPING AND BAKING THE BREAD

1. Grease a large baking sheet. Punch down dough; divide in half. Shape each half into a 12-inch-long oval.

2. Transfer loaves to the prepared baking sheet, placing them at least 2 inches apart. Let rise until almost doubled in size, about 30 minutes.

3. Preheat oven to 375°F. In a small bowl, beat egg white and water; brush each loaf with egg wash. Using a large sharp knife, make 3 diagonal slashes, about ½ inch deep, in each loaf. ▼

4. Divide Parmesan in half. Sprinkle each loaf with half of Parmesan. Bake loaves until they are golden brown and sound hollow when tapped, about 35 minutes. Transfer loaves to wire racks; cool completely.

Cool It

As soon as the potato bread comes out of the oven, transfer it to a cooling rack. This lets the steam escape, preventing the bread from becoming soggy and creating a crispy crust on all sides.

Pack it Pretty

Even a plain loaf of bread looks appealing when it's packed in a pretty basket. Craft stores sell beautiful French ribbon, which is wired to hold loops and curls. Try using soft, earthy colors—they complement the golden crust of this potato bread.

GOOD IDEA This recipe makes two loaves, so give one to a friend and keep the other one for your family's supper.

Variations

Potato Stamp

Offer this bread with a potato-stamped card! Cut a potato in half; cut designs in it to look like bread. Use a light brown ink or watercolor to stamp onto kraft paper.

Chive Jive

A few fresh chives add a perky flavor to this bread. Add $1/2$ cup snipped fresh chives to the potato puree, then proceed with the recipe as directed.

Savory Pesto Swirls

You Will Need

FOR THE FILLING
- 1/3 **cup dry white wine or water**
- 1 **package (1 ounce) dry-packed sun-dried tomatoes**
- 2 **tablespoons prepared pesto**
- 3 **tablespoons mayonnaise**

FOR THE DOUGH
- 1 **package (8 ounces) refrigerated crescent rolls**

MAKES 1 DOZEN ROLLS

**BAKING TIME
13 MINUTES**

Kitchen Tips
You can prepare the swirls up to 1 day ahead; wrap well in plastic wrap and refrigerate. Bake just before serving.

PREPARING THE FILLING

1. In a small bowl, combine wine and sun-dried tomatoes; let stand until tomatoes are softened, about 30 minutes.

2. Drain tomatoes; chop coarsely. In a blender or a food processor fitted with a metal blade, combine tomatoes and pesto; process, stopping to scrape the sides of the bowl as needed, until a fine paste forms, less than 1 minute.

3. Transfer the paste to a medium bowl. Add mayonnaise; mix well.

BAKING THE ROLLS

1. Preheat oven to 375°F. Unroll the dough on a flat work surface (it will be approximately 12 x 8 inches). Press the perforated lines together. ▼

2. Spread the pesto mixture evenly over dough. Starting with a short side, roll up dough jelly-roll style. ▼

3. Using a serrated knife, cut roll into 12 equal slices; place on an ungreased baking sheet, 2 inches apart. ▼

4. Bake rolls until golden brown, about 13 minutes. Serve warm.

Attention to Detail

Come up with other fillings for these versatile rolls! Try these flavorful ideas:

• Cheddar cheese, mustard and thyme • Tapenade (olive paste) • Monterey Jack cheese, green chiles and cilantro • Caramelized onions, Parmesan cheese and sage

Great for Guests

For company, fill the swirls with several different fillings for a "wow" presentation. You can assemble them a day ahead and bake just before serving.

Sweet Switch

These swirls also taste great with a sweet filling—try using a cinnamon-nut paste for a satisfying snack.

Tasty Sauce

The filling for this recipe makes a zesty new dressing for your potato, chicken or pasta salad. To use as dressing, increase the mayonnaise to $1/2$ cup.

GOOD IDEA Roll the edges of the baked swirls in melted butter, then in chopped fresh herbs for a fresh look and taste!

Variations

Shape Up

For another flavorful, filled shape, spoon the pesto filling into pastry squares and fold the corners toward the center; bake as recipe directs.

Quick Crescents

Make it easy! Separate the prepared dough along the perforations; unroll each crescent and spread the filling along the wide end. Roll up and bake as directed.

Bagel Bread

You Will Need

🌿🌿🌿

FOR THE BREAD

- 6 cups all-purpose flour, divided
- 3 tablespoons sugar
- 1 tablespoon salt
- 1½ packages (1 tablespoon) active dry yeast
- 2 cups warm water (105°F-110°F)

FOR THE TOPPING

- 1 teaspoon poppy seeds
- 1 teaspoon sesame seeds
- 1 teaspoon dried minced garlic
- 1 teaspoon dried minced onion
- 1 egg white
- 1 teaspoon water

SPECIAL AIDS

two 8- x 4-inch loaf pans

MAKES 2 LOAVES

BAKING TIME
35 MINUTES plus rising

Kitchen Tips

- For the best flavor, choose unbleached all-purpose flour for this recipe.
- If seeds brown too quickly, cover bread with foil during the last 10 minutes of baking time.

MAKING THE DOUGH

1. Grease a large bowl. In another large bowl, using an electric mixer set on low speed, combine 2 cups flour, sugar, salt and yeast; beat until combined. Add water; beat on medium speed until dough is smooth and elastic, about 5 minutes.

2. Add 3 more cups flour, ½ cup at a time, beating well after each addition.

3. Turn dough onto a lightly floured surface. Knead, adding remaining flour a little at a time, until incorporated and dough is smooth, about 5 minutes. ▼

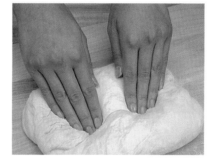

4. Transfer dough to the prepared bowl, turning to coat. Cover with oiled plastic wrap; set in a warm place for 30 minutes. (Dough will rise but will not be doubled in size.)

5. Preheat oven to 375°F. Grease two 8- x 4-inch loaf pans. Punch down dough; divide in half. Working with 1 piece of dough at a time, knead until smooth and elastic, about 2 minutes.

6. Pat dough into a 10- x 4-inch rectangle. Starting at 1 short end,

roll up dough, jelly-roll style; pinch seam and ends to seal. ▼

7. Place roll, seam-side down, in the prepared pan. Repeat with remaining dough. Cover pans with oiled plastic wrap. Let dough rise until it reaches pan top, about 20 minutes; remove plastic.

TOPPING & BAKING THE LOAVES

1. In a small bowl, combine poppy seeds and sesame seeds. In another small bowl, combine garlic and onion. In a third small bowl, whisk egg white and water until frothy, about 1 minute. Brush loaves with egg wash. Sprinkle 1 topping mixture onto each loaf. ▼

2. Bake loaves until browned, about 35 minutes. Let bread cool completely.

Toast It

Just like a bagel, this bread is crisp on the outside, slightly chewy on the inside and at its best when toasted.

By Hand

If your mixer is not a heavy-duty model, mix up the dough with a wooden spoon and a lot of elbow grease—just as Grandma did. Set a slightly damp folded towel under the bowl to stabilize it.

Storage Tip

Because this bread has no added fat, it can go stale quickly. If you do not plan to eat it the day it's baked, wrap it tightly and freeze.

GOOD IDEA Slice this bagel bread thin; toast and cut into triangles to make canapés. Top with cream cheese and smoked salmon.

Variations

Cream-Cheese Spread

Love cream cheese on your bagels? Make a tasty spread: Blend cream cheese and butter, then add sliced green onions or chopped fresh herbs.

Flavored Swirl Loaves

Sprinkle a tablespoon of topping ingredients onto a dough rectangle; roll and set in a loaf pan. Add remaining topping and bake as directed.

Banana-Pecan Bread

MAKING THE BREAD

1. Preheat oven to 350°F. Grease and lightly flour a 9- x 5-inch loaf pan.

2. In a large heavy-bottomed skillet, toast pecans over medium heat, stirring occasionally, until lightly browned, 3-5 minutes. ▼

3. In a large bowl, combine all-purpose flour, wheat flour, granulated sugar, baking powder, baking soda and salt. Stir in toasted pecans; set aside.

4. In a medium bowl, using a fork, mash bananas. ▼

5. Add butter, eggs, milk and brown sugar to bananas; mix well.

6. Add banana mixture to flour mixture; stir until moistened.

7. Spoon batter into prepared pan. Bake bread for 45 minutes; tent with aluminum foil. Continue baking until bread is browned and a wooden skewer inserted into the center comes out clean, about 30 minutes longer. ▼

8. Transfer the pan to a wire rack; cool for 10 minutes. Turn the bread onto the wire rack; cool completely.

Attention to Detail

For another fun version of this recipe, convert it into banana-pecan muffins:

BANANA-PECAN MUFFINS

1. Grease and lightly flour 12 standard muffin pan cups.

2. Spoon batter into cups, filling them just to the top.

3. Bake muffins until a toothpick inserted in center comes out clean, 25-30 minutes. Transfer the pan to a wire rack; cool for 10 minutes. Turn muffins onto rack; cool completely.

Chocolate Chunk

For a taste almost everyone will love, replace the pecans with ½ cup semisweet chocolate chips.

Crack Up

Don't worry if the top of your bread cracks during baking; this shows the batter has expanded properly.

Stock Up

To store this bread, wrap it in plastic wrap and then aluminum foil; freeze for up to 3 months. When you have company or are planning a special breakfast, thaw the frozen bread in the refrigerator overnight.

GOOD IDEA For gourmet "banana splits," serve slices of this bread on pools of chocolate syrup; top with vanilla ice cream.

Variations

Sweet Banana Muffins
For a quick snack, prepare batter with chocolate chips, pour into a muffin pan and bake about 30 minutes.

Chocolate Banana Loaf
Transform this bread into a sweet dessert! Pour your favorite chocolate icing over the loaf; top with chopped pecans.

Chocolate Chip Crumb Cakes

You Will Need

✿✿✿✿✿

FOR THE TOPPING

⅓	cup all-purpose flour
⅓	cup sugar
¼	teaspoon cinnamon
¼	cup (½ stick) butter or margarine, chilled

FOR THE CRUMBCAKES

2	cups all-purpose flour
⅓	cup sugar
I	tablespoon baking powder
½	teaspoon salt
I	large egg
I	cup milk
3	tablespoons butter, melted
I	cup mini semisweet chocolate chips

MAKES 12 CRUMBCAKES

**BAKING TIME
25-30 MINUTES**

Kitchen Tips

Make sure you mix in the chocolate chips thoroughly, or they will sink to the bottom of the crumbcake batter.

PREPARING THE TOPPING

1. In a small bowl, mix flour, sugar and cinnamon. Using a pastry blender or 2 knives, cut in butter until coarse crumbs form; set aside.

MAKING THE CRUMBCAKES

1. Preheat oven to 400°F. Grease and flour a 12-cup muffin pan.

2. In a large bowl, mix flour, sugar, baking powder and salt. In a medium bowl, beat egg, milk and melted butter. Pour egg mixture into flour mixture; stir until dry ingredients are moistened. Add chocolate chips; mix well. ▼

3. Fill prepared muffin cups about three-quarters full with batter. ▼

4. Sprinkle crumb topping on top of each crumbcake. ▼

5. Bake crumbcakes until lightly browned, 25-30 minutes.

Attention to Detail

You can easily vary the flavor of these crumbcakes. Just add any of the following ingredients to the batter before baking:

- ¼ teaspoon almond extract
- ½ cup dried cherries
- ½ cup dried cranberries
- ½ cup dried currants

Or, change the flavor of the topping. Instead of cinnamon, add one of these ingredients:

- ¼ cup flaked coconut
- crushed chocolate wafers
- ⅓ cup sliced almonds
- grated orange peel

Easy Substitute

For a richer cake with a more delicate texture, substitute 1 cup of sour cream for the milk.

Chip Change

Try this recipe with peanut butter or butterscotch chips instead of chocolate. Or, you can replace half of the chocolate chips with $\frac{1}{2}$ cup crushed toffee bar.

Sweet Topping

To sweeten these crumbcakes, make a glaze with $\frac{1}{4}$ cup confectioners' sugar and a little milk; drizzle over the crumbcake topping.

GOOD IDEA Wrap up these crumbcakes and pack them into bags or lunch boxes for a special midday treat.

Variations

Double Chocolate

For chocolate lovers, mix 2 ounces melted semisweet chocolate into the batter. Fold in chocolate chips; continue as recipe directs. Drizzle with additional melted chocolate.

Supersize It

For one large crumbcake, pour batter into a greased and floured 8-inch tart pan with removable bottom. Sprinkle with topping; bake at 350°F. for 45-50 minutes.

Graham Nut Bread

You Will Need

FOR THE BREAD

- 2 cups graham flour
- 1 cup chopped walnuts
- ½ cup all-purpose flour
- ¼ cup firmly packed dark brown sugar
- 1 teaspoon baking powder
- 1 teaspoon baking soda
- 1 teaspoon salt
- ¼ cup vegetable shortening
- 1½ cups buttermilk
- ½ cup molasses

FOR THE FROSTING AND GARNISH

- 2 packages (3 ounces each) cream cheese, softened
- ¼ cup confectioners' sugar
- 3 tablespoons plain yogurt
- 2 tablespoons finely grated orange zest (zest from 1 large orange)
- 1 orange

SPECIAL AIDS

citrus stripper
small offset spatula

MAKES I LOAF

**BAKING TIME
50 MINUTES**

Kitchen Tips

To reduce cracking on the top of the bread, let the batter stand in the pan for 20 minutes before baking.

MAKING THE BREAD

1. Preheat oven to 375°F. Grease a 9- x 5-inch loaf pan. In a large bowl, combine graham flour, walnuts, all-purpose flour, brown sugar, baking powder, baking soda and salt.

2. In a small saucepan, melt shortening over medium-low heat; remove the pan from heat. Add buttermilk and molasses; stir until well blended. Add buttermilk mixture to flour mixture; stir until well blended. ▼

3. Spoon batter into the prepared pan. Bake until a toothpick inserted in center comes out clean, about 50 minutes. Transfer the pan to a wire rack; cool for 5 minutes. Turn bread onto the rack; cool completely.

FROSTING AND GARNISHING THE BREAD

1. In a food processor fitted with a metal blade, combine cream cheese, confectioners' sugar, yogurt and orange zest; pulse once or twice, scraping down the sides of the bowl, until fluffy and well blended, about 2 minutes. ▼

2. Using a small offset spatula, spread frosting over top of bread, swirling top. Using a citrus stripper, remove several long strips from orange. Top bread with strips of orange zest; serve. ▼

Attention to Detail

Like all whole-wheat flours, graham flour has a higher fiber, nutritional and fat content than all-purpose flour. Because of their fat content, whole-wheat flours should be stored in the refrigerator to prevent spoilage.

Good Graham

Graham flour, which is whole-wheat flour containing the bran of the wheat kernel, got its name from the Rev. Sylvester Graham. He advocated the use of whole-grain flours for healthful baking. The graham cracker was also named after him.

Spread Joy

Instead of frosting the bread after baking, serve the frosting on the side as a spread.

Make Ahead

The bread may be frozen, in a resealable plastic bag, for up to 1 month. Frost it just before serving.

GOOD IDEA This old-fashioned bread is the perfect item to include ina basket to welcome a new family to the neighborhood.

Variations

Graham Nut Muffins

To enjoy this distinctive taste in a muffin, bake the batter in lined muffin pans for 15-20 minutes at 375°F. Top with piped frosting stars.

Raisin Boost

Add fruit flavor to this old-time bread. Stir ²/₃ cup raisins into the batter with the nuts; bake as directed. Garnish with a confectioners' sugar glaze.

Magic Cookie Dough Muffins

You Will Need

FOR THE MUFFINS

- 1 roll (18 ounces) refrigerated chocolate chip cookie dough, at room temperature
- 2 packages (3 ounces each) cream cheese, cut into small pieces
- 1 can (14 ounces) sweetened condensed milk
- ¾ teaspoon baking powder
- ½ cup chopped walnuts or pecans
- ½ cup raisins

FOR THE TOPPINGS

- ⅔ cup sweetened coconut
- ⅔ cup dried cherries
- ¾ cup finely chopped walnuts

SPECIAL AIDS

- one 12-cup muffin pan
- one 6-cup muffin pan
- paper or foil muffin cup liners

MAKES 16 MUFFINS

**BAKING TIME
25-30 MINUTES**

Kitchen Tips

Adding 2-3 tablespoons water to any unused muffin cups will keep the pan from warping.

MAKING THE MUFFINS

1. Preheat oven to 350°F. Line 16 muffin cups with paper or foil liners.

2. In a medium bowl, using an electric mixer set on medium speed, beat cookie dough until fluffy, about 1 minute. ▼

3. Add cream cheese to dough; beat until blended, about 1 minute. ▼

4. Add condensed milk, baking powder, walnuts and raisins to dough; beat until blended, about 1 minute.

5. Spoon batter into the prepared muffin cups, filling each cup about three-quarters full. Add 2-3 tablespoons water to the 2 unfilled muffin cups.

6. Top 5 muffin cups with coconut, 5 cups with dried cherries and 6 cups with chopped walnuts. ▼

7. Bake muffins until tops are golden brown, 25-30 minutes. Transfer the pans to wire racks; cool for 2 minutes. Turn muffins onto the racks; cool completely.

Attention to Detail

MIX 'N' MATCH MUFFINS

Customize this quick and easy muffin recipe—just add 1 cup of any of these ingredients to your muffin batter in place of the nuts and raisins:

- chopped peeled apples
- chopped pitted dates
- peanut butter chips
- mini candy-coated chocolates
- butterscotch chips
- white chocolate pieces
- dried cranberries
- granola
- chopped dried apricots
- toffee candy pieces

Classic Flavors

Try these quick and easy muffins with your favorite variety of refrigerated cookie dough, such as sugar or peanut butter.

From Scratch

Using store-bought cookie dough makes this recipe super-simple, but you can also use the dough from any chocolate chip cookie recipe.

The Best Part

If the crunchy tops are your favorite part of any muffin, try using a muffin-top pan. This muffin batter will fill 24 of the wide, shallow cups in these pans.

GOOD IDEA Make your batch like traditional magic cookies: Sprinkle a combo of all the toppings onto each muffin.

Variations

Magic Coffee Cake

This versatile dough makes a great coffee cake, too! Just bake it in a greased 9-inch square pan for 25 minutes, then drizzle with a glaze of melted chocolate.

Snow-Capped Muffins

Transform this afternoon snack into a yummy dessert with a layer of frosting. Cream cheese frosting perfectly complements the sweetness of these muffins.

Candied Cookie Box

You Will Need

❧❧❧❧❧

FOR THE COOKIES

1 package (18 ounces) refrigerated sugar cookie dough

½ cup all-purpose flour

FOR THE ICING

powdered egg whites (equivalent to 4 fresh egg whites)

1 package (1 pound) confectioners' sugar

2 teaspoons lemon juice

assorted food coloring

SPECIAL AIDS

2½-inch round cookie cutter

small resealable plastic bags

MAKES 3 DOZEN COOKIES

FOR THE CANDY BOX

small cardboard box

white paper or gift wrap

tape

hot glue gun and glue sticks

assorted round starlight candies

assorted stick candies

tissue paper

**BAKING TIME
8-10 MINUTES**

Kitchen Tips

To save time, frost cookies with one color icing and add dots with food coloring gel. Using the tip of a knife, swirl the gel through the icing.

MAKING THE COOKIES

1. Preheat oven to 350°F. In a large bowl, combine cookie dough with flour. On a lightly floured surface, roll dough to a ¼-inch thickness. Using a cookie cutter, cut the dough into 2½-inch rounds; transfer cookies to ungreased baking sheets. Bake the cookies for 8-10 minutes. Transfer cookies to wire racks to cool.

DECORATING THE COOKIES

1. In a medium bowl, prepare egg whites according to package directions. Using an electric mixer set on high speed, beat in confectioners' sugar and lemon juice until smooth. If necessary, add a few drops of hot water to create a thick glaze.

2. Divide icing among several bowls. Stir in assorted food coloring, 1 drop at a time, to create desired colors. Spoon some of each icing into separate resealable plastic bags; snip off one corner.

3. Spread each cookie with one color of icing; pipe dots of a contrasting color around the outer edge. Using the tip of a knife, pull the dots of color toward the center in a "C" shape. ▼

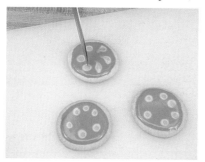

4. Drag your finger clockwise around the outer edge of the cookie to pull the icing into a swirl pattern. ▼

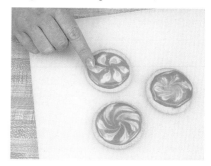

5. Repeat icing process with remaining cookies. Let stand until icing is set, at least 30 minutes.

MAKING THE CANDY BOX

1. Wrap the box with white paper; affix with tape.

2. Using a hot glue gun, attach the round starlight candies and stick candies to the paper-covered box in desired patterns, covering the outside of the box completely. ▼

3. Line the box with tissue paper. Arrange the cookies inside.

All Occasion

You can change the look of this box and the cookies for any holiday. Use black and orange stick candies to create a Halloween box. Or, try making an all-green one for St. Patrick's Day.

Candy Crush

For more color, crush different colored stick candies and sprinkle on the cookies before the icing sets.

Box Treat

To make this candy box edible, keep the candies in their wrappers or attach unwrapped candies with frosting.

GOOD IDEA Offer this festive box of cookies as a holiday gift and tie on a red licorice-whip bow for real candy store ambiance.

Variations

Candy Cane Box

To make a nifty holiday container to hold cookies or a small gift, wrap a coffee can with white paper and glue on candy canes.

Penny Candy Cookies

For a different look, cut dough into wrapped penny candy shapes. After baking and frosting, use white icing to pipe on the "wrapper."

Checker Box Cookies

You Will Need

❧❦❧❦❧

FOR THE COOKIE DOUGH

- 1 **cup butter, softened**
- 2 **teaspoons vanilla extract**
- 1⅓ **cups light brown sugar**
- ½ **cup granulated sugar**
- 2 **large eggs, beaten**
- 3 **cups all-purpose flour**
- ½ **teaspoon cream of tartar**
- ½ **teaspoon salt**
- 2 **squares (2 ounces) semi-sweet chocolate, melted and cooled**

MAKES 6 DOZEN COOKIES

FOR THE CHECKERBOARD BOX

- 2 **12-inch squares red construction paper**
- 1 **12-inch square sturdy cardboard**
- **ruler**
- **pencil**
- **black broad-tipped marking pen**
- **nontoxic glue**
- **clear plastic wrap**
- 1 **12-inch flat box**
- **ribbon**

**BAKING TIME
10 MINUTES**

MAKING THE COOKIE DOUGH

1. In a large bowl, using an electric mixer set on low speed, beat together butter, vanilla, brown sugar and granulated sugar. Add beaten egg; mix well.

2. In another bowl, sift together flour, cream of tartar and salt.

3. Using an electric mixer set on low speed, beat flour mixture into butter mixture until blended.

4. Divide dough in half; add melted chocolate to one half; mix well.

5. Place each dough half on a large square of waxed paper. Form each into a log about 1 inch in diameter; roll in the waxed paper on a flat surface to smooth as much as possible. Twist ends of paper. Refrigerate dough for 2 hours or overnight until thoroughly chilled. ▼

MAKING THE COOKIES

1. Preheat oven to 350°F. Unwrap rolls carefully to retain their shape; quickly slice into ¼-inch-thick rounds. Place on ungreased baking sheets and bake until vanilla cookies are lightly browned and chocolate cookies are dark brown, about 10 minutes. Transfer to wire racks and cool completely.

MAKING THE CHECKERBOARD BOX

1. Trim red construction paper and cardboard to fit inside the box. Using the ruler and pencil, draw a grid of 1½-inch squares, 8 squares by 8 squares, on the paper.

2. Using marking pen, fill in squares to form checkerboard pattern. ▼

3. Glue checkerboard to cardboard. Wrap checkerboard in plastic wrap, pulling edges of plastic wrap tightly around back of cardboard to form a smooth surface.

4. Glue second sheet of construction paper over back of checkerboard to secure plastic wrap. Place inside box.

5. Stack each flavor of cookie separately and wrap each in plastic wrap; tie at the ends with ribbon. Arrange in the box.

Get on Board

To play a game of "checkers," arrange chocolate cookies on three rows of black squares at one side of the board and put vanilla cookies on three rows of black squares on the other side. Leave two empty rows in the middle of the board as the playing area.

Baker's Tip

When making these vanilla and chocolate cookies, it's best to check them often after the first few minutes of baking to be sure they don't brown too quickly.

■ **GOOD IDEA**

Offer these as a gift to friends who like board games. Play a game and let them eat each piece they capture!

Variations

Citrus Flavor

Add zing to chocolate cookies by adding 1 tablespoon finely grated orange peel, use ¹/₂ teaspoon orange extract for the vanilla and omit cinnamon.

Traveler's Checker Box

Make a mini checker box using a 6-inch square box. Roll dough ¹/₂ inch in diameter; cut slices ¹/₈ inch thick. Bake for 5 minutes.

Chocolate-Dipped Pirouettes

You Will Need

❧❧❧❧

FOR THE COOKIES

¼ cup (½ stick) butter, softened

½ cup plus 2 tablespoons confectioners' sugar

2 egg whites at room temperature, slightly beaten

½ teaspoon vanilla extract

⅛ teaspoon salt

¼ cup plus 3 tablespoons cake flour

3 squares (3 ounces) semisweet or bittersweet chocolate

SPECIAL AIDS

thin offset spatula

waxed paper

MAKES ABOUT 1 DOZEN COOKIES

BAKING TIME
45–50 MINUTES

Kitchen Tips

• To help ensure that this light batter does not separate, bring all ingredients to room temperature (70°F.). If the butter, sugar and egg mixture curdles, don't worry; beat it on high speed for 1 minute before adding the flour. If it continues to separate, add another teaspoon of flour and mix well.

• Because the edges of a cookie usually bake faster than the center, spread the batter as evenly as possible.

MAKING THE DOUGH

1. Preheat oven to 350°F. Lay a clean dish towel on work surface.

2. In a small bowl, using an electric mixer set on medium speed, beat butter until it is light and fluffy. Add the confectioners' sugar a little at a time, mixing well after each addition. Add the egg whites in 3-4 additions, mixing well after each. Add vanilla and beat on high for 30 seconds.

3. Using a spatula, stir in the salt. Add the flour, 2 tablespoons at a time, mixing well after each addition.

FORMING THE COOKIES

1. Place a mounded tablespoon of batter on a nonstick baking sheet. Using an offset spatula, spread the batter into a very thin, even round about 4½ inches in diameter. Repeat with one more cookie. Bake until cookies are brown around the edges and lightly golden in the center, about 6 minutes. ▼

2. Using a spatula, very quickly loosen 1 cookie from the baking sheet. Turn cookie upside down on a work towel.

3. With the top side facing down, roll the cookie around the handle of a wooden spoon, forming a tight cylinder. Hold in place until the cookie shape is set. Remove spoon; transfer cookie to rack. Cool completely. ▼

4. Return second cookie to oven for 30 seconds to soften; repeat rolling process. Repeat with remaining cookies.

COATING THE COOKIES

1. Melt chocolate in top of a double boiler set over warm water. Hold one cookie at its center and dip each end in melted chocolate. Place on a sheet of waxed paper to set; repeat with remaining cookies.

Classic Cups

For a unique and stylish way to serve these sophisticated cookies, lay one pirouette across the rim of a cup of freshly brewed coffee.

Crisp Contrast

Pirouettes make a wonderful crispy contrast when served with ice cream or sorbet. Stick a couple of cookies into a scoop for a fun presentation.

Storage Tip

To keep them fresh, store these delightful cookies in airtight containers.

GOOD IDEA Wrap pirouettes in cellophane, tie with ribbon and tuck into a pretty coffee cup for a co-worker's birthday.

Variations

Crispy Dessert Cups

These edible cups make great bowls for a fresh berry dessert. Mold warm cookies on the bottom of a custard cup. Let cool and enjoy!

Chocolate Pirouettes

For an even sweeter treat, spread melted chocolate on each warm cookie, roll it up and dip ends in chocolate. Serve with ice cream.

Chocolate-Glazed Shortbread

You Will Need

❧❧❧❧

FOR THE SHORTBREAD

- 1 cup plus 2 tablespoons all-purpose flour
- 1/3 cup confectioners' sugar
- 1/2 cup (1 stick) butter, softened

FOR THE GLAZE

- 1/3 cup milk chocolate chips
- 1/2 teaspoon vegetable oil

SPECIAL AIDS

pastry blender

small resealable plastic bag

MAKES 20 COOKIES

**BAKING TIME
25 MINUTES**

Kitchen Tips

- You can substitute 1/3 cup rice flour for an equal amount of all-purpose flour. Because rice flour does not contain gluten (a protein that produces a chewy texture), it creates a shortbread that's more tender and crumbly.

- For perfect wedges, it is important to cut shortbread twice—once before baking and again while it is still warm. If the shortbread has cooled completely before the second cut, it will break apart.

MAKING THE SHORTBREAD

1. Preheat oven to 325°F. In a medium bowl, combine flour and sugar. Using a pastry blender or 2 knives, cut in butter until coarse crumbs form. Gently knead the mixture until dough forms.

2. On an ungreased baking sheet, pat dough into a 10- x 3½-inch rectangle. Using a long knife, cut dough crosswise into 1-inch strips; do not separate pieces. Cut each piece in half diagonally, again cutting through to bottom but not separating pieces. ▼

3. Using a fork, prick each piece of shortbread 3-4 times. ▼

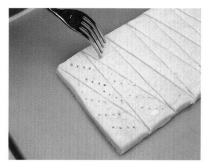

4. Bake shortbread until the bottoms of the wedges are just starting to brown, about 25 minutes. Transfer the pan to a wire rack, cut pieces apart and let cool for 5 minutes. Transfer shortbread to a wire rack; cool completely.

5. Combine chocolate chips and oil in a small microwave-safe bowl. Microwave on MEDIUM until chocolate melts, about 2 minutes. Spoon the melted chocolate into a small plastic bag; snip off one corner. Pipe chocolate over shortbread as desired. ▼

Attention to Detail

Purists demand that shortbread contain only three ingredients: butter, sugar and flour. But this tasty tradition is a wonderful starting point for variations. Try adding any of these to the dough:

- 1 teaspoon lemon juice or grated lemon peel
- 2 tablespoons finely chopped toasted nuts
- 1/2 teaspoon vanilla extract
- 1/4 cup mini chocolate chips
- 1/4 cup finely chopped dried fruits, such as cranberries or raisins

Straighten Up

To create straight edges and squared corners on your shortbread, pat the dough against a ruler when shaping it.

It's a Snap

To make shortbread "fingers," pat the dough into an 8- x 6-inch rectangle; then cut into 2- x 1-inch rectangles. Bake them on ungreased baking sheets.

Sweet Tip

If you prefer an even sweeter treat, sift confectioners' sugar over cooled cookies or sprinkle them with cinnamon sugar.

GOOD IDEA Instead of using chocolate, drizzle these cookies with another flavor, such as a raspberry or strawberry glaze.

Variations

Short & Sweet Gift

For a lovely and delicious present, give shortbread baked in a traditional mold—the classic way to make shortbread. Tie it with a ribbon.

Dipped Shortbread

For the chocolate lover, cut the shortbread with a round cookie cutter; bake, then dip half of each cookie into melted chocolate.

Chocolate Swirl Crisps

MAKING THE COOKIE DOUGH

1. In a large bowl, combine flour, baking powder and baking soda; mix well. Set flour mixture aside.

2. In another bowl, using an electric mixer set on medium speed, beat together sugar, maple syrup, margarine and vanilla. Beat in egg whites. Reserve 3/4 cup batter.

3. On low speed, beat 1 1/2 cups flour mixture into remaining batter until a soft dough forms; set aside.

4. In a medium bowl, beat together reserved batter, remaining flour mixture and cocoa until a soft dough forms. Shape each dough half into a log; wrap in waxed paper and chill for 30 minutes.

SHAPING THE COOKIES

1. Roll out each log between 2 sheets of waxed paper into an 1/8-inch-thick rectangle. Remove top sheet of waxed paper from both rectangles. Place one dough rectangle directly on top of the other rectangle. ▼

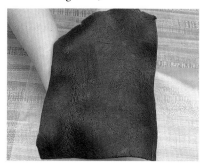

2. Starting at one end, roll up layered dough, removing waxed paper as it rolls. Wrap rolled dough in waxed paper and chill for about 2 hours. ▼

3. Preheat oven to 350°F. Spray 2 baking sheets with vegetable cooking spray. Cut the dough crosswise into 1/4-inch-thick slices; place slices 2 inches apart on prepared baking sheets. ▼

4. Bake cookies until golden, about 15 minutes. Transfer cookies to wire racks and cool.

Party Gift

These cookies will be a hit with adults as well as kids. Wrap a few cookies in clear cellophane and tie with a pretty ribbon to give as party gifts.

Make Ahead

Prepare the dough as recipe directs. Wrap in plastic wrap and refrigerate for up to 2 days. Then, just slice the dough when you are ready to bake.

Giant Bites

Double the recipe and roll it up in one log and you will have giant-sized cookies that are fun to eat.

GOOD IDEA Add a pinch or two of ground cinnamon to the chocolate dough for a pleasant flavor.

Variations

Pretty in Pink

Add a few drops of red food coloring or cranberry juice to the vanilla dough. Knead until evenly distributed to create a pink cookie dough.

Square Deal

To create square swirls instead of circles, roll dough as directed. Before slicing, shape dough log into square sides.

Cow Spot Cookies

You Will Need

❧❧❧

FOR THE COOKIES

- 8 ounces white chocolate candy melts (about 1½ cups)
- 2 tablespoons vegetable oil, divided
- 24 chocolate sandwich cookies (2-inch diameter)
- 8 ounces milk or dark chocolate candy melts (about 1½ cups)

SPECIAL AIDS

tongs
small resealable plastic bags

MAKES 2 DOZEN COOKIES

PREPARATION TIME
20 MINUTES plus chilling

Kitchen Tips

- White chocolate will scorch and clump if it is overheated, so watch it carefully when melting in the microwave.
- To protect the design on these cookies, store them in a single layer or stack them between sheets of waxed paper in an airtight container.

DECORATING THE COOKIES

1. Line 2 baking sheets with waxed paper. In a 2-cup glass measuring cup, combine white chocolate candy melts and 1 tablespoon oil. Microwave on HIGH for 1 minute; stir until smooth and melted.

2. Using tongs, dip a cookie into the melted white chocolate; tap off excess coating. Transfer cookie to a prepared baking sheet. Repeat for a total of 12 cookies. Chill until chocolate is set, about 20 minutes. Set aside remaining white coating. ▼

3. In another 2-cup glass measuring cup, combine milk chocolate candy melts and remaining oil. Microwave on HIGH for 1 minute; stir until smooth and melted.

4. Dip remaining cookies in melted milk chocolate; transfer to a prepared baking sheet. Chill until set, about 20 minutes. Set aside remaining milk chocolate coating.

5. When the chocolate is firm, lift the dipped cookies from waxed paper. Using a small knife, trim off any excess chocolate. ▼

6. Reheat reserved milk chocolate in the microwave on HIGH, stirring at 15-second intervals, until smooth. Transfer milk chocolate to a resealable plastic bag; snip off 1 corner. Pipe milk chocolate cow spots onto white chocolate-coated cookies. Chill cookies until spots are set, about 10 minutes. ▼

7. Repeat previous step with reserved white chocolate to decorate the milk chocolate-coated cookies.

Carefree Cookie

If you're on the "moo-ve," these are the perfect cookies for you! Just use any store-bought cookies, dip 'em in chocolate and decorate.

Quick & Easy

The candy melts used here are found at craft and party supply stores. Once set, the coating is firm and won't melt when touched as baking chocolate does.

Play Ball

Delight your sports fan— decorate these cookies to resemble soccer balls, baseballs or basketballs.

GOOD IDEA Use this method to design cookies with other animal prints—try zebra, tiger, giraffe or leopard!

Variations

Cow Talk

Give these cookies a voice of their own! Once the spot design is set, pipe "Moo" in bright red decorator's icing on top of each cookie.

Cow Spot Gift Bag

To match the theme, cover a milk carton with white paper and glue on black paper cow spots. Fill the decorated carton with cookies.

Edible Cookie Bowl

You Will Need

❧❧❧

FOR THE COOKIES

1¼	cups all-purpose flour
½	cup unsweetened cocoa powder
¼	cup blanched, slivered almonds, finely ground
½	teaspoon salt
4	tablespoons (½ stick) butter, softened
⅔	cup sugar
1	egg
½	teaspoon vanilla extract
	assorted cookies

SPECIAL AIDS

loaf pan
1½-inch cookie cutter with scalloped edges

MAKES 1 COOKIE BOWL

**BAKING TIME
15 MINUTES**

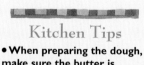

Kitchen Tips

- When preparing the dough, make sure the butter is completely softened so the dough will reach the proper consistency.

- To keep the dough from becoming too dry, use as little flour as possible when rerolling scraps for additional cookie shapes.

MAKING THE COOKIE DOUGH

1. Cover the outside of a loaf pan with foil. Spray with vegetable cooking spray.

2. In a medium bowl, combine flour, cocoa powder, almonds and salt. In a large bowl, using an electric mixer set on medium, beat butter, sugar, egg and vanilla until light and fluffy. Add flour mixture; beat until a dough forms, about 2 minutes.

SHAPING THE COOKIE BOWL

1. Preheat oven to 350° F. Roll dough out to ⅛-inch thickness. Using a 1½-inch cookie cutter with scalloped edges, cut out shapes. ▼

2. Cover pan with cutouts, overlapping and pressing them slightly. ▼

BAKING THE COOKIE BOWL

1. Bake cookie bowl until edges are firm, about 15 minutes. Transfer pan to a wire rack and cool completely.

2. To remove the cookie bowl, carefully lift it off the foil-lined loaf pan. Remove foil. ▼

3. Arrange other cookies in the cookie bowl. Cover loosely with plastic wrap until ready to serve.

Attention to Detail

Make a round cookie bowl by overlapping and molding the cookie dough disks over a round bowl. Use different shaped ovenproof bowls to make a varied selection of cookie bowls.

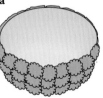

Kid Stuff

Instead of a cookie bowl, make individual cookies to fill the cookie jar. Prepare the dough as recipe directs. Shape into 1-inch balls. Place balls, 2 inches apart, on cookie sheets. Flatten slightly. Bake until edges are firm, about 10 minutes.

Freezer Option

Wrap the cooled cookie bowl in an airtight enclosure of plastic wrap; store in the freezer for up to 1 month. Thaw bowl, wrapped, at room temperature for about 30 minutes.

GOOD IDEA Bake a few smaller cookie bowls and serve with ice cream for a fun dessert treat.

Variations

A Candy Dish

For a delicious touch, fill a small cookie bowl with little chocolate candies.

All Wrapped Up

Offer a cookie bowl as a gift. Wrap in colorful cellophane paper and tie with ribbon.

Malted Milk Ball Cookies

You Will Need

❧❧❧❧❧

FOR THE COOKIES

1	cup chocolate-covered malted milk balls, divided
1¼	cups all-purpose flour
¼	cup malted milk powder
1	tablespoon unsweetened cocoa powder
½	teaspoon baking soda
⅔	cup sugar
½	cup (1 stick) butter or margarine, softened
1	egg
1	package (11½ ounces) milk chocolate chips, divided

MAKES ABOUT 3 DOZEN COOKIES

BAKING TIME
8-10 MINUTES plus standing

Kitchen Tips

• You can find malted milk powder in the beverage aisle of the grocery store. It comes in both plain and chocolate flavors. Try the chocolate version in this recipe for an extra chocolate boost.

• To avoid scorching the bottoms of these cookies, arrange the racks in the middle and upper half of the oven.

MAKING THE COOKIES

1. Using a large knife, coarsely chop ½ cup malted milk balls; set aside. Finely chop remaining malted milk balls. ▼

2. Preheat oven to 375°F. In a medium bowl, combine flour, malted milk powder, cocoa and baking soda.

3. In another medium bowl, using an electric mixer set on high speed, beat sugar and butter until fluffy. Beat in egg. With the mixer set on low, beat in flour mixture until a dough forms. Stir in coarsely chopped milk balls and ⅔ cup chocolate chips.

4. Using your hands, form dough into ¾-inch balls. Place balls of dough 1 inch apart on ungreased baking sheets. ▼

5. Bake cookies until edges are set, 8-10 minutes. Transfer the baking sheets to wire racks; cool for 1 minute. Transfer cookies to wire racks; cool completely.

FROSTING THE COOKIES

1. In a small microwave-safe bowl, microwave remaining milk chocolate chips on HIGH for 1 minute; stir until smooth and melted.

2. Dip cookies into melted chocolate to coat halfway; dip coated edges into reserved chopped malted milk balls. Let cookies stand until chocolate is firm, about 45 minutes. ▼

Attention to Detail

PACKAGE PRIMER

For an easy gift presentation, you can modify a gift bag, available at gift and card shops, to tote these cookies.

Using scissors, cut partway along each corner of a decorative gift bag to create flaps to fold over the top. Use pinking shears to trim the top edges. Fill with cookies; then fold over the top flaps and seal with a bow.

Flavor Fave

Wait 'til your friends get a load of these cookies— they'll get a blast from the past! Using malted milk powder and malted milk balls in a basic chocolate cookie dough recreates a flavor favorite from days gone by.

Nostalgia Night

The '50s are a "keen" party theme! Have a hula hoop contest, spin some rock 'n' roll hits and show the movie *Grease* or *Bye-Bye Birdie*. Refresh your guests with burgers, milk shakes, root beer floats and these nifty cookies.

GOOD IDEA For a different garnish, spread tops with melted chocolate, then nestle a halved malted milk ball on each cookie.

Variations

Fountain Favorite

Don't forget about the classic malted milk treat—a malted milk shake! Make it with vanilla ice cream; top with whipped cream and chopped malted milk balls.

Malted Milk Ball Mania

Assemble this fun '50s-era gift: Find a vintage napkin holder at an antique shop or tag sale and fill it with a hefty supply of malted milk balls.

Namesake Cookies

You Will Need

❦❦❦

FOR THE COOKIES

1	cup sugar
½	cup (1 stick) butter or margarine, softened
1	egg
1½	squares (1½ ounces) unsweetened chocolate, melted
1	teaspoon vanilla extract
¼	teaspoon almond extract
1½	cups all-purpose flour
¼	teaspoon salt
3	squares (3 ounces) white chocolate

SPECIAL AIDS

waxed paper

MAKES ABOUT 2 DOZEN COOKIES

**BAKING TIME
10-12 MINUTES**

Kitchen Tips

• To make sure these cookies don't fall apart, use a large spatula to carefully remove the hot cookies from the baking sheet.

• All ovens have hot and cool spots. If you're baking more than one sheet of cookies at a time, ensure even browning by rotating baking sheets from top to bottom and front to back halfway through baking time.

MAKING THE COOKIES

1. Preheat oven to 350°F. Grease a large baking sheet. In a large bowl, using an electric mixer set on high speed, beat sugar and butter until fluffy. Stir in egg, unsweetened chocolate and vanilla and almond extracts; beat until smooth.

2. With the mixer set on low speed, mix in flour and salt; continue beating until a soft dough forms.

3. Turn the dough onto a floured surface. Remove chunks of dough and roll into ¼-inch-thick ropes. ▼

4. Form dough into letters, each about 3 inches high, on the baking sheet. ▼

5. Bake cookies 10-12 minutes. Using a large spatula, carefully transfer cookies to a wire rack; cool completely.

6. Line a baking sheet with waxed paper. In a small microwave-safe bowl, heat white chocolate on MEDIUM for 2 minutes; stir to melt completely. Dip the bottoms of the cookies into the melted chocolate; place on a lined baking sheet until chocolate is cool. ▼

Attention to Detail

MELTING CHOCOLATE

• When melted in the microwave, chocolate holds its shape rather than melting into a puddle. For this reason, you can melt chocolate squares right in their paper wrapping.

• Melted chocolate should be allowed to come to room temperature before it is added to the other ingredients. This prevents warm chocolate from cooking the egg and melting the butter, both of which would change the texture of the cookie batter.

ABCs

Making these cookies is a great project to do with children. They can spell out their names, simple words or create the whole alphabet. Try shaping numbers, too!

Puzzle Present

Give someone the gift of a cookie puzzle to work out. Select a word, like friendship, congratulations or devotion, and arrange the scrambled letters in a gift box. Then, let him or her know on the gift card that an anagram is enclosed. Figuring out the word will be part of the fun!

■ **GOOD IDEA** Shape these cookies into Xs and Os and send your loved one a box filled with tasty hugs and kisses !

Variations

Colorful Cookies

For more color and crunch, coat these cookies entirely in melted white chocolate, then decorate them with sprinkles or colored sugar.

Special Message

Use your imagination! Make cookies that express a holiday greeting, a special sentiment or even a phrase that only you and your friend will understand!

Peanut Butter & Jelly Cookies

You Will Need

FOR THE COOKIES

- ½ cup (1 stick) butter, softened
- ½ cup creamy peanut butter
- ½ cup firmly packed light brown sugar
- ¼ cup granulated sugar
- 1 large egg
- ½ teaspoon vanilla extract
- 1 cup all-purpose flour
- ½ teaspoon salt
- ½ teaspoon baking soda
- ¼ cup seedless raspberry jam

MAKES ABOUT 3 DOZEN COOKIES

BAKING TIME 10-12 MINUTES

Kitchen Tips

- To cream butter with other ingredients by hand, press them against the side of the bowl with a wooden spoon.

- Let cookies cool 1 minute before removing them from the pan. This gives them time to become firm.

- When the recipe makes more cookies than will fit on the number of baking sheets you have, line the sheets with aluminum foil. While the first batch is baking, form the next cookies on additional foil sheets. When the first batch comes out of the oven, slide the foil onto the cooling rack, and place the foil with the unbaked cookies onto the baking sheet.

MAKING THE COOKIE DOUGH

1. Preheat oven to 350°F. In a large bowl, using an electric mixer set on low speed, cream together butter, peanut butter, brown sugar and granulated sugar; mix well. Add egg and vanilla; mix until smooth, scraping down sides of the bowl with a rubber spatula.

2. In a large bowl, sift together flour, salt and baking soda. Stir into butter mixture until completely blended. ▼

BAKING THE COOKIES

1. Form dough into 1-inch balls and smooth with fingers or drop by tablespoonfuls onto an ungreased baking sheet; flatten with thumb, making a small well in the center of each one. ▼

2. Drop about ½ teaspoon of jam onto the center of each cookie. ▼

3. Bake cookies until lightly browned around the edges, 10-12 minutes. Let cookies cool 1 minute on baking sheet. Transfer to wire rack to cool completely.

Attention to Detail

Peanut butter and jelly is a classic taste combination. But you can fill those little wells with other flavors that are sure to please. For chocolate lovers, bake the cookies unfilled, let cool and then add this easy filling:

CHOCOLATE FILLING

- ¾ cup chocolate chips
- 1 tablespoon butter or margarine
- 1½ tablespoons corn syrup
- 2 teaspoons water
- 1 teaspoon vanilla

In top of double boiler set over warm water, melt chocolate chips, butter, corn syrup and water. Stir in vanilla. Let cool for 5 minutes. Fill cooled cookies with chocolate filling.

Freezing Tip

To keep these fragile, buttery cookies from breaking while in storage, set them close together on a baking sheet and freeze. Pack frozen cookies carefully in tightly sealed plastic containers and return to the freezer.

Child's Play

Kids love to help bake these fun cookies. Pressing their thumb into the dough is usually their favorite part! Be sure to let your assistant choose the jam flavor to use as filling.

GOOD IDEA Use a variety of fruit jams—blueberry, peach, apricot, pear—for a colorful and tasty presentation.

Variations

Peanut Power

Give these cookies extra crunch and a more nutty flavor by sprinkling chopped dry-roasted peanuts over the jam filling before baking.

Sandwich Cookies

Recreate this classic sandwich combination. Add $3/4$ cup oatmeal to batter and bake; choose your favorite jam to layer between cookies.

Rainbow Cookies

You Will Need

FOR THE COOKIES

1   cup (2 sticks) butter or margarine, softened
2   cups sugar
2   large eggs
1½ teaspoons vanilla extract
½   teaspoon almond extract
4½ cups all-purpose flour
1   tablespoon baking powder
¼   teaspoon salt
red, yellow, green and blue food coloring pastes
1   cup prepared vanilla frosting
white nonpareils

SPECIAL AIDS

ruler
scalloped flower cookie cutter

MAKES 2½ DOZEN COOKIES

BAKING TIME
20 MINUTES

Kitchen Tips

• If you're short on time, use refrigerated cookie dough. For the amount of dough needed in this recipe, use 2 packages (18 ounces each) sugar cookie dough mixed with 1 cup flour.

• You can place decorated cookies in the refrigerator for a few minutes to set the frosting quickly. However, the finished cookies are best stored at room temperature.

MAKING THE COOKIES

1. In a large bowl, using an electric mixer set on medium speed, beat butter and sugar until fluffy. With mixer on low speed, beat in eggs and vanilla and almond extracts. Beat in flour, baking powder and salt until a dough forms.

2. Measure ¼ cup dough; knead in red food coloring until desired color is reached. Roll into a 5-inch log.

3. Measure ½ cup dough; knead in yellow food coloring. Roll dough into a 5- x 3½-inch rectangle; use a ruler to keep the corners square. Place red log in center; fold yellow dough around log. Pinch to seal (do not overlap edges). Roll to form a smooth 5-inch log.

4. Measure ¾ cup dough; knead in green food coloring. Roll dough into a 6- x 5-inch rectangle. Place log in center; fold green dough around log. Pinch to seal; roll to form a 5-inch log. ▼

5. Measure 1 cup dough; knead in blue food coloring. Roll into a 8½- x 5-inch rectangle. Place log in center; fold blue dough around log, pinching to seal edges.

Roll to form a smooth log; wrap in waxed paper. Freeze until firm, about 1 hour, rolling log every 15 minutes.

6. Preheat oven to 350°F. Grease 3 baking sheets. Roll remaining dough to a ¼-inch thickness. Use a scalloped flower cookie cutter to cut clouds. ▼

7. Transfer cloud cookies to prepared baking sheets; bake for 8 minutes. Transfer cookies to wire racks to cool.

8. Cut log in half lengthwise along seam; cut each half into 15 slices. ▼

9. Bake cookies about 10 minutes. Let cool. Frost clouds with vanilla frosting; place a rainbow cookie on each. Sprinkle with nonpareils; let stand to set frosting.

Smile Makers

These cookies make people smile! Deliver a bunch to a friend who is feeling under the weather for a quick pick-me-up.

Cloud Shapes

If you don't have a scalloped-edge flower cookie cutter, use a small round one and overlap several rounds to form each cloud—or try cutting clouds freehand.

Party Plan

Love classic movies? Rent *The Wizard of Oz*, make these cookies and invite friends to an "Over the Rainbow" party!

■ **GOOD IDEA** Serve these at a birthday party with a rainbow and unicorn theme. Give magic wands as favors!

Variations

Pot of Gold

These are a real crowd pleaser! Frost cupcakes in white; insert a rainbow cookie in the cupcake and add a gold foil-covered candy at one end of the rainbow.

Piped Rainbows

For a quick fix, form prepared cookie dough into a 3-inch diameter roll; freeze and slice. Cut each slice in half. Bake as directed; decorate with frosting.

White Chocolate Blondies

BAKING THE BLONDIES

1. Preheat oven to 325°F. Line a 9-inch square baking pan with aluminum foil so the foil extends a few inches over 2 sides of the pan. Spray the foil with vegetable cooking spray.

2. In a small bowl, combine flour, baking powder and salt; set aside. In a medium bowl, using an electric mixer set on medium speed, beat light brown sugar and butter until smooth, about 3 minutes. Using a wooden spoon, add eggs, egg yolk and vanilla and almond extracts to the butter mixture.

3. With the mixer on low speed, beat flour mixture into butter mixture.

4. Using a wooden spoon, stir nuts and ½ cup white chocolate chips into the dough; mix well. ▼

5. Spread dough evenly in the prepared pan; bake blondies until a toothpick inserted in center comes out clean, about 35 minutes. Transfer the pan to a wire rack; cool completely.

6. Using the foil overhangs as handles, lift blondies out of the pan. Carefully remove all the foil; transfer blondies to a cutting board. Cut blondies into 16 squares, then cut each square in half diagonally to form 32 triangles. ▼

7. Place confectioners' sugar in a fine mesh sieve; sift sugar over the blondies.

8. Place remaining white chocolate chips in a small microwave-safe bowl. Microwave chocolate on MEDIUM, about 45 seconds; stir until chocolate is smooth and melted. Using a fork, drizzle the melted white chocolate over the blondies. Let the blondies stand until the chocolate is set. ▼

Maple Blondies

The sweet flavor of maple goes well with the macadamia nuts in these bar cookies. For a taste sensation, replace the almond extract with maple extract and use butterscotch chips or chopped walnuts instead of white chocolate chips.

Care Package

These soft blondies mail well. Pack them closely together in a sturdy box, coffee can or cardboard milk container; place the container inside a box and surround with crumpled paper or foam "popcorn."

■ **GOOD IDEA** For a romantic treat, cut the blondies with a heart-shaped cookie cutter and decorate with candy hearts.

Variations

Choco-Chip Blondies

For a twist on the classic chocolate chip cookie, use semisweet mini chocolate chips in the batter instead. Cut into squares and serve plain.

Blond Brownie Sundae

These blondies make a super base for an ice-cream dessert. Skip the sugar and glaze; layer brownies with ice cream and top with hot caramel sauce.

Carrot Cake

You Will Need

FOR THE CAKE

- 2 cups all-purpose flour
- 2 teaspoons baking soda
- 2 teaspoons ground cinnamon
- 1/2 teaspoon salt
- 4 large eggs
- 1 1/2 cups granulated sugar
- 1 cup vegetable oil
- 3 cups grated carrots

FOR THE FROSTING

- 1 package (8 ounces) cream cheese
- 1/4 cup (1/2 stick) butter or margarine, softened
- 3 cups confectioners' sugar
- 1 cup chopped pecans

FOR THE MARZIPAN CARROTS

- 1/2 cup (half of 7-ounce tube) marzipan or almond paste, divided
  red, yellow and green food coloring

SERVES 12

BAKING TIME
30-35 MINUTES

Kitchen Tips

To make orange marzipan for the carrots, start with yellow food coloring. Then add red food coloring, one drop at a time, until the desired color is reached.

MAKING THE CAKE

1. Preheat oven to 350°F. Grease and flour two 9-inch round cake pans. In a medium bowl, combine flour, baking soda, cinnamon and salt.

2. In a large bowl, combine eggs, sugar and oil; mix well. Stir in flour mixture until smooth; add carrots. Pour batter into pans. ▼

3. Bake until a toothpick inserted in center comes out clean, 30-35 minutes. Place pans on wire rack; cool for 10 minutes. Run a knife around sides to loosen cake layers and then turn onto wire rack; cool completely.

MAKING THE FROSTING

1. In a large bowl, using an electric mixer set on medium-high speed, beat cream cheese and butter until fluffy. On low speed, gradually beat in confectioners' sugar.

2. Cover the cake layers with frosting.

MAKING THE CARROTS

1. In a small bowl, mix a small amount of red and yellow food coloring with 1/4 cup marzipan to make orange. Tint another 1/4 cup marzipan green. On a sheet of waxed paper, shape 10-12 carrots with tops.

DECORATING THE CAKE

1. Arrange carrots on top of cake. Coat sides of cake with pecans. Refrigerate until ready to serve. ▼

Attention to Detail

Change the look of the finished product by placing marzipan carrots around the top edge of the cake.

Smart Idea

Showcase this cake—make it a colorful centerpiece for your Easter dinner or buffet table.

Fresh Keeping

Since this is a moist cake, it is important to store it in the refrigerator. If it is tightly covered with plastic wrap, it will keep for several days.

Cut the Fat

If you're looking to cut calories, try using low-fat or fat-free cream cheese in the frosting. Look for it in the dairy case at your supermarket.

■ **GOOD IDEA** Turn this cake into muffins and dust with cinnamon and sugar before baking. Serve at your next brunch.

Variations

Sweet Simplicity

For less fuss, add $1/2$ cup each raisins and chopped nuts to the batter. Bake in a rectangular pan and dust the top with confectioners' sugar.

Layered Look

Divide cake batter among three 8-inch pans. Bake, cool and spread the top of each layer with a walnut- or pecan-filled frosting.

Brownie Baked Alaska

You Will Need

✦✦✦✦✦

FOR THE BROWNIE

¾ cup butter or margarine

½ cup unsweetened cocoa powder

1¼ cups sugar

3 large eggs

1½ teaspoons vanilla extract

¾ cup all-purpose flour

FOR THE FILLING

2 pints coffee ice cream

1 pint vanilla ice cream

FOR THE MERINGUE

4 large egg whites

¼ teaspoon cream of tartar

½ cup sugar

SERVES 10

BAKING TIME
30-35 MINUTES

Kitchen Tips

• Take care when separating eggs. Just a little bit of yolk in the egg whites will keep them from becoming stiff for the meringue.

• Cream of tartar prevents problems associated with overbeating, a common cause of meringue shrinkage during the baking period.

MAKING THE BROWNIE

1. Preheat oven to 350°F. Line a 9-inch round cake pan with foil; grease foil. In a medium saucepan, melt butter over low heat. Remove from heat. Whisk in cocoa until smooth; let mixture cool. Add sugar, eggs and vanilla to saucepan; stir in flour. Spoon batter into prepared pan.

2. Bake until a toothpick inserted in center comes out clean, 30-35 minutes. Place pan on wire rack; cool completely. Lift brownie out of pan and turn onto a heatproof serving plate or a small baking sheet; remove foil.

LAYERING THE FILLING

1. Let the ice cream soften slightly. Cover the brownie with 1 pint coffee ice cream; shape into a dome. Repeat with vanilla ice cream and remaining coffee ice cream. Use the back of a spoon to smooth the ice cream. Freeze until ice cream is solid, about 2 hours. ▼

MAKING THE MERINGUE

1. Preheat oven to 425°F. In a large bowl, using an electric mixer set on high speed, beat egg whites until foamy. Add cream of tartar and beat until soft peaks form. Gradually add sugar, beating until stiff peaks form. ▼

2. Spread meringue over ice cream and brownie to cover completely. Bake in upper third of oven just until meringue begins to brown, 4-6 minutes. Serve immediately. ▼

Attention to Detail

For a picture-perfect meringue, start with egg whites at room temperature. Use a clean bowl (copper is best) and clean, grease-free beaters.

Sauce It

Warm your favorite chocolate sauce and serve alongside this pretty dessert.

Favorite Flavor

Let your family choose their favorite ice cream flavors for the Baked Alaska. They'll definitely ask for seconds.

Soften Up

If you don't have time to let the ice cream soften at room temperature, warm it in a microwave for 3-second intervals until it's easy to spread. Check the ice cream after each interval.

GOOD IDEA For true coffee lovers, stir 2½ teaspoons instant espresso powder into the sugar for the meringue.

Variations

Mini Baked Alaska

Serve these at your next party. Prepare brownies in a 9-inch square pan. Cut into squares, top as usual and finish with whipped cream and cocoa.

Keep Cool

For a no-bake version, omit brownie, cover the ice cream with whipped topping and dust lightly with unsweetened cocoa powder.

Cherry Upside-Down Cake

You Will Need

ᏋᏋᏋᏋᏋ

FOR THE TOPPING

- ⅔ cup firmly packed light brown sugar
- 2 tablespoons (¼ stick) butter or margarine, melted
- 20 large sweet cherries (about ¾ pound), stemmed, halved and pitted
- ½ cup pecan halves

FOR THE CAKE

- 1 cup cake flour
- 1½ teaspoons baking powder
- ⅛ teaspoon salt
- 2 extra-large eggs, separated
- ½ cup granulated sugar
- 5 tablespoons hot water
- 1 teaspoon vanilla extract
- ½ teaspoon almond extract

SERVES 8

**BAKING TIME
35 MINUTES**

Kitchen Tips

- Canned pitted cherries can be substituted for the fresh cherries in this recipe, but they must be very well drained and patted dry.
- Use pan protector strips to insulate the pan and keep cake level and moist; they can be purchased at most specialty kitchen shops.

ARRANGING THE TOPPING

1. Preheat oven to 350°F. Generously grease a 9-inch round cake pan.

2. In a small bowl, combine brown sugar and butter; sprinkle mixture evenly over the bottom of the prepared pan. Alternately place cherries, cut-side up, and pecans in a spiral pattern. ▼

PREPARING THE BATTER

1. In a small bowl, sift flour, baking powder and salt; set aside. In a medium bowl, using an electric mixer set on medium speed, beat egg yolks; add sugar, a little at a time. Beat mixture until thick and lemon-colored, about 4 minutes.

2. Alternately add water and flour mixture to batter, beating after each addition. Add vanilla and almond extracts; beat until smooth, about 1½ minutes longer.

3. In another medium bowl, using clean beaters, beat the egg whites on medium-high speed until stiff peaks form, about 4 minutes. Using a rubber spatula, gently fold the egg whites into the batter just until incorporated.

4. Spoon batter into the pan, being careful not to disturb the topping; gently smooth top. ▼

BAKING THE CAKE

1. Bake cake on the middle oven rack until top is golden brown and springs back when pressed with a finger, about 35 minutes. Transfer the pan to a wire rack; let cool for 10 minutes.

2. Run a small sharp knife around the edges of the pan. Place a serving plate over the pan; invert pan and carefully turn cake onto the serving plate. Serve cake warm.

Attention to Detail

HOW TO PIT A CHERRY

Insert a small sharp knife into the cherry, moving the knife around the pit in a circular motion; then, halve the cherry. Twist halves gently to easily separate cherry from pit; remove pit.

À la Mode

A dollop of whipped cream or a dainty scoop of French vanilla ice cream accents this treat beautifully.

Vary Cherries

Make this delectable cake with a variety of cherries. Choose red, yellow and dark purple in peak cherry season. Later, use well-drained canned cherries.

Autumn Cake

For a fabulous fall or holiday cake, replace cherries with 2 cups fresh red cranberries. Arrange the berries on the brown sugar mixture and proceed as directed.

GOOD IDEA Throw a "life-is-a-bowl-of-cherries" party to celebrate a happy event. Look for paper goods with a cherry theme.

Variations

Cake 'n' Custard

To give your cake a restaurant-worthy presentation, serve each piece on a pool of vanilla custard or crème anglaise.

Chocolate Cherries

Dip fresh cherries in melted chocolate and use them to garnish cake plates or to encircle the platter.

Chocolate Cake Roll

You Will Need

❧❧❧❧❧

FOR THE CAKE

- 1/3 cup cake flour
- 1/3 cup unsweetened cocoa powder
- 2 tablespoons cornstarch
- 1/2 teaspoon baking soda
- 1/2 teaspoon baking powder
- 1/3 teaspoon salt
- 4 large eggs, separated
- 1 cup granulated sugar, divided

confectioners' sugar

FOR THE FILLING

- 1 container (8 ounces) frozen whipped topping, thawed

SERVES 10

**COOKING TIME
15 MINUTES**

Kitchen Tips

- For easier slicing, place cake in freezer 20 minutes before you're ready to serve.
- Use a large serrated knife and a gentle sawing motion to slice the cake cleanly.

MAKING THE CAKE

1. Preheat oven to 350°F. Line a 15- x 10-inch jelly roll pan with waxed paper. Grease and flour lined pan; tap out excess.

2. In a medium bowl, combine flour, cocoa powder, cornstarch, baking soda, baking powder and salt. Mix well. In a separate bowl, using an electric mixer set on medium speed, beat egg yolks and 1/4 cup sugar until fluffy.

3. In a small bowl, using clean beaters, beat egg whites on high until foamy. Gradually add 1/2 cup sugar, beating until stiff, but not dry, peaks form.

4. Fold 1/3 beaten egg whites into egg yolk mixture. Alternately fold in remaining whites and flour mixture. Pour batter in pan; smooth top. Bake until a toothpick inserted in center comes out clean, about 15 minutes.

ROLLING AND FILLING THE CAKE

1. Dust a clean cloth with remaining sugar. Turn cake out onto prepared cloth; remove waxed paper. Trim the cake's edges. ▼

2. Starting with a long side, tightly roll up cake with cloth. Transfer cake, seam-side down, to a wire rack to cool. ▼

3. Unroll cake; remove cloth. Spread whipped topping over cake to within 1/2 inch of edges. Re-roll cake; place seam-side down on a plate. Dust with confectioners' sugar before serving. ▼

Attention to Detail

Mix some mini chocolate morsels into the filling before spreading on the cake for a chocolaty surprise.

Simple Switch

Turn this cake into a frozen treat by filling with ice cream. Spread softened ice cream over cake. Roll as directed and wrap well. Freeze cake, seam-side down, until firm. Slice and serve with chocolate sauce.

Easy Fill

For a sweeter cake, try jelly, canned pie fillings or pudding as a cake filler.

Fun with Fruit

Fresh berries or chopped fruit mixed into the cream filling add an elegant touch.

GOOD IDEA Pipe a name or a message onto the side of the cake for a personal touch.

Variations

Serving Suggestion
Place a slice of this cake over a pool of chocolate sauce. Serve with a sprig of mint and some fresh raspberries for a tasty treat.

For Chocolate Lovers
Chocolate and coffee are an unbeatable duo. Just add cooled melted chocolate and instant coffee granules to this luscious filling.

Decadent Chocolate Cake

You Will Need

FOR THE CAKE

- ½ cup dark corn syrup
- ½ cup (1 stick) butter or margarine
- 1 cup semisweet chocolate morsels
- ½ cup sugar
- 3 large eggs, lightly beaten
- 1 teaspoon vanilla extract
- 1 cup all-purpose flour
- 1 cup chopped pecans or walnuts

FOR THE CHOCOLATE GLAZE

- ⅔ cup semisweet chocolate morsels
- ¼ cup dark corn syrup
- 2 tablespoons butter or margarine
- 2 teaspoons whipping cream

FOR THE CHOCOLATE LEAVES

- 2 squares (2 ounces) semisweet chocolate, coarsely chopped
- 8 lemon leaves

SERVES 10

**BAKING TIME
30 MINUTES**

Kitchen Tips

Toasting nuts for 6-8 minutes before adding them to the batter helps to bring out their fullest flavor.

MAKING THE CAKE

1. Preheat oven to 350°F. Grease a 9-inch round cake pan. In a saucepan, combine corn syrup and butter; bring to a boil. Stir in chocolate morsels. Remove from heat.

2. In a medium bowl, combine sugar, eggs and vanilla; stir into chocolate mixture. In another bowl, combine flour and nuts; add to chocolate mixture.

3. Pour batter into prepared pan; smooth top. Bake cake until a toothpick inserted in center comes out clean, about 30 minutes. Transfer pan to a wire rack and cool for 10 minutes. Turn cake onto rack and cool completely.

MAKING THE GLAZE

1. In a saucepan, melt chocolate, corn syrup and butter over low heat; stir in cream. Pour glaze over cooled cake.

MAKING THE CHOCOLATE LEAVES

1. Line a baking sheet with waxed paper. In the top of a double boiler set over simmering, not boiling, water, melt chocolate. Paint chocolate over one side of each lemon leaf. ▼

2. Place leaves, chocolate-side up, on prepared baking sheet. Chill until set.

3. Gently peel each leaf away from the chocolate. ▼

4. Arrange chocolate leaves around edge of cake. ▼

Attention to Detail

For a more elaborate cake, arrange the chocolate leaves in an overlapping pattern around the top of the cake and add a center of fresh raspberries.

Make Ahead

The chocolate leaves can be prepared in advance and stored in the refrigerator for up to 1 day.

Go-Withs

Serve this cake with chocolate whipped cream. Just combine 2 tablespoons each unsweetened cocoa powder and confectioners' sugar with 1 cup heavy cream. Beat until soft peaks form.

Quick Change

Decorate the top of the cake with chocolate curls instead of leaves.

GOOD IDEA This rich dessert is the perfect birthday cake for any chocolate lover.

Variations

One-Bite Delight

Because of its richness, this cake is perfect for making petit fours. Just bake the cake in a square pan; cut into small squares, glaze and decorate.

Quick Design

Instead of adding a glaze, arrange leaf stencils on top of cooled cake; sprinkle with confectioners' sugar, then remove stencils to reveal design.

Oatmeal Cookie Cake

You Will Need

FOR THE CAKE

1⅓	cups old-fashioned rolled oats
1¾	cups boiling water
1	cup granulated sugar
1	cup firmly packed light brown sugar
⅔	cup butter
3	eggs
1½	teaspoons vanilla extract
1⅔	cups all-purpose flour
1½	teaspoons baking soda
1	teaspoon cinnamon
¾	teaspoon ground ginger
½	teaspoon salt
¾	cup raisins

FOR THE FILLING

1¼	cups vanilla frosting (from a 16-ounce can)
2	teaspoons cinnamon

FOR THE GLAZE

1	cup confectioners' sugar
2-3	tablespoons milk
2	tablespoons chopped walnuts

SPECIAL AIDS

small resealable plastic bag

SERVES 12

**BAKING TIME
30-35 MINUTES**

BAKING THE CAKE

1. Preheat oven to 350°F. Grease and flour two 9-inch round cake pans. In a medium bowl, combine oatmeal and water; let soak until oatmeal is softened and water is absorbed, 15-20 minutes.

2. In a small bowl, combine granulated sugar and brown sugar. In a large bowl, using an electric mixer set on medium, beat butter into sugar mixture, a little at a time, until light and fluffy, about 4 minutes. Add eggs, one at a time, beating after each addition; add vanilla. Beat in oatmeal mixture until combined.

3. In a small bowl, sift flour, baking soda, cinnamon, ginger and salt. With the mixer set on low speed, alternately add flour mixture and raisins to batter; beat until blended, about 2 minutes. Divide batter between the prepared pans.

4. Bake until a toothpick inserted in centers comes out clean, 30-35 minutes. Transfer the pans to a wire rack; cool for 10 minutes. Turn cakes onto the rack; cool completely.

MAKING THE FILLING

1. In a small bowl, using an electric mixer set on medium speed, combine frosting and cinnamon. Beat filling until blended, about 1 minute; set aside.

MAKING THE GLAZE

1. In a medium bowl, using an electric mixer set on medium speed, combine confectioners' sugar and 2 tablespoons milk; beat mixture until smooth, about 1 minute. Add more milk, if necessary, to reach desired consistency; set aside. ▼

ASSEMBLING THE CAKE

1. Place 1 cake layer on a serving platter; cover top with filling. Place second cake layer on top of filling.

2. Spoon glaze into a small resealable plastic bag. Snip off 1 corner of the bag; drizzle glaze over cake in a sunburst pattern, starting in center and moving out toward the edges. ▼

3. Just before serving, place walnuts in center of glaze.

Oatmeal Loaf

This batter makes a tasty pound cake and a perfect portable gift. Bake it in a loaf pan, wrap it in a tea towel and take the glaze along in a jar.

Cherry Choice

Sweet cherries add a new flavor and a bit of color to this cake. Sprinkle well-drained maraschino or pitted Bing cherry halves over both top and bottom cake layers.

À la Mode

Sophisticate this cake! Just top a slice with a big scoop of butter pecan or rum raisin ice cream.

GOOD IDEA Indulge your sweet tooth: Have a slice of this oatmeal cake for breakfast instead of the usual bowl of cereal.

Variations

Daisy Muffins

Give your morning a sunny start with these cheerful muffins. Drizzle on glaze "petals" and sprinkle chopped nuts in the centers.

Made with Love

Turn store-bought oatmeal cookies into a favorite childhood treat with a coat of sweet icing. Use the glaze in this recipe for traditional crisscross strokes.

Tomato Soup Cake

You Will Need

FOR THE CAKE

- 1¼ cups granulated sugar
- ½ cup (1 stick) butter or margarine, softened
- 2 large eggs, beaten
- 1 teaspoon cinnamon
- 1 teaspoon ground nutmeg
- ½ teaspoon ground cloves
- ½ teaspoon salt
- 2 cups all-purpose flour
- 1 teaspoon baking powder
- 1 cup dried currants
- 1 can (10 ounces) condensed tomato soup
- 1 teaspoon baking soda

FOR THE FROSTING

- 3 cups confectioners' sugar
- 2 packages (8 ounces each) cream cheese, softened
- 2 teaspoons vanilla extract

red and orange colored sugar

SPECIAL AIDS

small offset spatula

pastry bag fitted with a medium round tip

SERVES 8

BAKING TIME
30-35 MINUTES

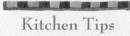

Kitchen Tips

For level, moist and evenly browned cakes, rotate the cake pans in the oven or use cake strips, which can be found at specialty kitchen shops.

MAKING THE CAKE

1. Preheat oven to 375°F. Grease and lightly flour two 8-inch round cake pans.

2. In a large bowl, using an electric mixer set on medium speed, beat sugar and butter until light and fluffy, about 2 minutes. Add eggs and beat 1 minute longer. Add cinnamon, nutmeg, cloves and salt; beat until combined.

3. With the mixer set on low, add flour and baking powder, a little at a time, beating until smooth and well blended, about 2 minutes. (The dough will be stiff.) Beat in currants. ▼

4. In a small bowl, combine tomato soup and baking soda; add to batter, stirring until combined. ▼

5. Divide batter evenly between the prepared pans. Bake cakes on the middle oven rack until a toothpick inserted in centers comes out clean, 30-35 minutes.

6. Transfer pans to a wire rack; cool for 10 minutes. Turn cakes onto the rack; cool completely.

MAKING THE FROSTING

1. In a medium bowl, using an electric mixer set on medium-low speed, beat confectioners' sugar, cream cheese and vanilla until fluffy, about 3 minutes.

ASSEMBLING AND DECORATING THE CAKE

1. Place 1 cake layer on a serving plate, flat-side down; using a small offset spatula, spread with frosting. Top with remaining cake layer, flat-side up. ▼

2. Frost top and sides of cake. Spoon remaining frosting into a pastry bag fitted with a medium round tip.

3. Pipe a decorative border around top and bottom edges of cake. Sprinkle red and orange colored sugar over piped borders; serve.

Hot Tomato

Challenge your family to guess the surprise ingredient in this spicy cake—tomato soup! It adds moisture and a fruity, full flavor to this dessert.

Fruit and Nuts

If currants aren't your favorite fruit, use plain or golden raisins or dates in this cake. Toss in the chopped nuts of your choice, too.

Li'l Tomatoes

You can also bake this recipe as 24 cupcakes and decorate each one to look like a tomato: Spread the tops with red frosting and add a green-icing stem.

■ **GOOD IDEA** For an old-fashioned welcome home, serve this flavorful cake to finish your family's favorite meal.

Variations

Souper-Duper Dip

Here's another great use for canned soup: Mix 1 can of bean-and-bacon soup with ¹/₂ cup each sour cream and salsa. Serve it with veggies.

Souped-Up Favorite

Make easy macaroni and cheese: Stir 1 can Cheddar-cheese soup and 1 cup milk into 4 cups cooked pasta. Top with crumbs and bake until heated through.

Sweet Carrot Pie

You Will Need

❧❧❧❧❧

FOR THE CRUST

- 1 package (6 ounces) cornbread stuffing, finely ground (about 1⅓ cups)
- 6 tablespoons (¾ stick) butter, melted
- ⅓ cup granulated sugar

FOR THE FILLING

- 6 large carrots, peeled and cut into ¾-inch pieces (about 3 cups)
- ½ cup firmly packed dark brown sugar
- ½ cup granulated sugar
- 2 eggs, lightly beaten
- ¼ cup (½ stick) butter or margarine, softened
- ¼ cup honey
- 1½ teaspoons vanilla extract
- 1¼ teaspoons cinnamon
- 1 teaspoon ground nutmeg
- ½ teaspoon salt
- ¼ teaspoon ground cloves

FOR THE GARNISH

- 1 cup whipped cream
- ½ cup grated carrot
- ground nutmeg

SERVES 8

**BAKING TIME
55-60 MINUTES**

PREPARING THE CRUST

1. Preheat oven to 350°F. In a small bowl, combine stuffing, butter and sugar. Press mixture firmly into the bottom and sides of a 9-inch pie plate. ▼

MAKING THE FILLING

1. Place carrots in a medium saucepan, cover with water and cook over medium-high heat until fork-tender, about 30 minutes. In a colander, drain carrots.

2. Using a food processor fitted with a metal blade or a blender, process carrots until smooth; transfer carrot puree to a small bowl and set aside. ▼

3. In a large bowl, combine brown sugar and granulated sugar, stirring to blend; add carrot puree, eggs, butter, honey, vanilla, cinnamon, nutmeg, salt and cloves.

4. Using an electric mixer on medium speed, beat carrot mixture until smooth, about 2 minutes; pour mixture into prepared crust.

5. Bake until a toothpick inserted in center comes out clean, 55-60 minutes. Transfer to a wire rack to cool completely.

SERVING THE PIE

1. Cut pie into 8 slices; top each slice with 2 tablespoons whipped cream. ▼

2. Sprinkle pie slices with grated carrot and nutmeg; serve immediately.

Attention to Detail

There's no end to the delightful carrot-themed garnishes you can create for this pie.

Try shaping carrots from orange-tinted marzipan. Or, make carrot-shaped sugar cookies and sprinkle them with orange colored sugar.

cook's essentials step-by-step cookbook

Fall Flavors

Accompany this pie with a scoop of ginger ice cream. Or, whip up fresh cream and add a dash of cinnamon for a fall specialty.

Chill Out

Have some extra time on your hands? Bake and freeze a few of these pies for easy ready-made desserts to get a jump on the holidays.

Other Options

For a delicious change of taste, replace the carrots with canned pumpkin puree or pureed winter squash. Make a gingersnap-cookie crust, too.

GOOD IDEA Make this fall harvest pie as a reward for your family after the leaves are raked and the garden is put to bed.

Variations

Cider Sensation

Team this pie with a big pitcher of hot or chilled apple cider. Serve with cinnamon sticks for stirrers.

Creamy Carrots

Tint a little of this whipped cream green and the rest orange, then decorate the pie with piped-on carrots.

Chocolate Chess Pie

You Will Need

FOR THE CRUST

1½	cups all-purpose flour
2	tablespoons confectioners' sugar, sifted
½	teaspoon salt
½	cup (1 stick) cold butter, cut into small pieces
¼	cup vegetable shortening
¾	cup finely chopped pecans
¼	cup ice water

FOR THE FILLING

1¼	cups granulated sugar
3	tablespoons all-purpose flour
1¼	cups buttermilk
3	tablespoons unsweetened cocoa powder
2	tablespoons butter, melted and cooled
2	teaspoons vanilla extract
⅛	teaspoon salt
3	eggs plus 1 egg yolk, lightly beaten

FOR THE GARNISH

2	cups whipped cream
2	tablespoons chopped pecans

SPECIAL AIDS

pastry blender
9-inch ceramic or glass pie plate
pastry bag fitted with a star tip

SERVES 8

BAKING TIME
1 HOUR 15 MINUTES plus chilling

MAKING THE CRUST

1. In a large bowl, combine flour, confectioners' sugar and salt, stirring to combine. Add butter and shortening; toss to coat. Using a pastry blender or 2 knives, cut butter and shortening into flour mixture until coarse crumbs form. Add pecans; stir with a fork.

2. Add ice water, 1 tablespoon at a time, mixing with a fork until a soft dough forms. Gather dough into a ball. On a lightly floured surface, gently knead dough. Flatten dough into a disk; wrap in plastic wrap and refrigerate for at least 1 hour.

3. On a floured surface, using a floured rolling pin, roll dough into a 10-inch round. Drape dough over the rolling pin; transfer to a 9-inch pie plate, leaving a 1-inch overhang. Fold dough edges under; crimp edges. Chill until ready to use. ▼

MAKING THE FILLING

1. Preheat oven to 425°F. In a large bowl, using a whisk, combine sugar and flour. Add buttermilk, cocoa, butter, vanilla and salt; whisk until blended, about 1 minute. Add eggs; whisk until thoroughly combined, about 30 seconds longer. Pour filling into crust. ▼

BAKING & GARNISHING THE PIE

1. Transfer the pie plate to a baking sheet. Bake pie for 15 minutes. Reduce oven to 350°F. Bake until a toothpick inserted in center comes out clean, about 1 hour longer. Transfer the pie plate to a wire rack; cool completely.

2. Spoon whipped cream into a pastry bag fitted with a star tip. Pipe a ring of whipped cream around the inside edges of piecrust. ▼

3. Pipe a second ring of whipped cream in the center of pie. Sprinkle pecans over top of pie; serve.

Chess Pie

The classic Southern chess pie is made with a rich custard filling. This version includes pecans and chocolate for a tasty twist on the original recipe.

Citrus Pie

Add a little sunshine to your pie. Substitute 2½ teaspoons fresh lemon or lime juice and 1 teaspoon grated zest for the cocoa in this recipe.

Under Cover

Create a different look by covering the entire pie with fresh whipped cream and garnishing with chopped pecans or walnuts.

GOOD IDEA Serve this dessert to top off a Southern-inspired family-reunion menu that includes fried chicken and shrimp.

Variations

Classic Buttermilk

Just omit the cocoa powder from this recipe to make another traditional Southern favorite—buttermilk chess pie.

Chess Mate

To add flavor and color to your pie, spoon a pool of pureed raspberries onto each dessert plate. Top with fresh berries.

Sweet Lemon Pie

You Will Need

FOR THE CRUST

2½ cups all-purpose flour
¾ teaspoon salt
½ cup (1 stick) butter, chilled and cut into small pieces
½ cup vegetable shortening
6-8 tablespoons cold water
1 egg, beaten
yellow colored sugar

FOR THE FILLING

2 medium lemons, peel grated and reserved
2 cups granulated sugar
⅓ cup all-purpose flour
¼ teaspoon salt
3 tablespoons butter or margarine, melted
3 eggs
½ cup water

FOR THE GLAZE

½ cup confectioners' sugar
1 tablespoon freshly squeezed lemon juice

SPECIAL AIDS

pastry blender
9-inch pie plate

SERVES 10

BAKING TIME
45 MINUTES plus chilling

PREPARING THE DOUGH

1. In a large bowl, combine flour and salt. Using a pastry blender or 2 knives, cut in butter and shortening until mixture resembles coarse crumbs. Add water, 1 tablespoon at a time, until dough begins to clump together.

2. Divide dough in half; wrap each half in plastic wrap. Chill for 1 hour.

MAKING THE FILLING

1. Preheat oven to 400°F. Cut ends from peeled lemons. Stand each lemon on end on a work surface. Using a sharp knife, remove pith.

2. Thinly slice lemons; remove seeds. In a large bowl, whisk sugar, flour and salt until blended. Whisk in lemon peel, butter, eggs and water until blended. Stir in lemon slices. ▼

BAKING AND GLAZING THE PIE

1. On a floured surface, using a lightly floured rolling pin, roll half of dough into a 13-inch round. Fit dough into a 9-inch pie plate; trim edges to a ½-inch overhang. Roll remaining dough into a 13-inch round for the top crust.

2. Roll out dough scraps. Using a small sharp knife, cut out lemon shapes. ▼

3. Stir filling; pour into pie shell. Place top crust over filling; trim overhang to ¾ inch. Fold edges under bottom crust. Using your fingers, crimp and flute edges of crust. Cut vents in center of top crust.

4. Brush cutouts with beaten egg; place brushed-side down on top of pie. Brush tops of cutouts with remaining egg; sprinkle with yellow sugar. Bake pie until golden brown, about 45 minutes. Transfer to a wire rack; cool completely.

5. For the glaze, in a small bowl, combine confectioners' sugar and lemon juice. Drizzle glaze around cutouts; spread with the back of a spoon to smooth. Let pie stand until glaze is set.

Attention to Detail

If you don't have a citrus zester to grate the lemon peel, use the smallest holes of a box grater instead.

Tasty Toppings

For a new look, try placing lemon-slice candies around the edges of the pie or pipe lemon shapes with yellow icing.

Lemon Lovers

Crazy about lemons? Add even more of that great flavor by mixing 2 teaspoons grated lemon peel into the crust dough.

Flavor Trio

Go citrus! Make the glaze for this pie with lime juice instead of lemon and top it with orange-shaped pastry cutouts flavored with grated orange peel.

GOOD IDEA Serve each slice of this pie with a scoop of lemon sorbet and some lemon-flavored cookies!

Variations

Saucy Servings

Raspberry sauce is a great accompaniment to this pie. Make your own puree with fresh raspberries or use the ready-made variety.

Citrus Candles

To accent the table, line a small plate with lemon leaves, add a votive candle and decorate with mini artificial lemons.

Turtle Cream Pie

BAKING THE CRUST

1. Preheat oven to 450°F. Let piecrust stand at room temperature for about 15 minutes; peel off plastic sheets. Place crust in a 9-inch glass pie plate; press firmly against sides and bottom. Fold back excess crust; crimp and flute. Prick bottom and sides with fork. ▼

2. Bake until lightly browned, about 8 minutes. Transfer pie plate to a wire rack; cool completely.

MAKING THE FILLING

1. In a microwave-safe bowl, combine caramels and water. Microwave on HIGH at 1-minute intervals, stirring well after each interval, until mixture is smooth, 2-3 minutes. Let cool for 10 minutes.

2. In a large bowl, beat eggs with a fork. Add brown sugar, sour cream, pecans, vanilla and caramel mixture; mix well. Pour mixture into crust. Reduce oven heat to 350°F. Bake until filling is set, about 30 minutes. Transfer pie plate to wire rack; cool completely. Refrigerate until thoroughly chilled.

MAKING THE TOPPING

1. In a microwave-safe bowl, combine cream and milk chocolate chips. Microwave on HIGH for 1 minute; whisk until chips are melted and mixture is smooth. Cool to room temperature, about 1 hour. Using an electric mixer set on high speed, beat chocolate mixture just until it lightens in color; spoon over pie and spread to edges of crust. Refrigerate until firm, about 2 hours. ▼

2. Put white and semisweet chocolates in two small bowls over pans of simmering water; stir each until melted. Dip half of the pecans in white chocolate and half in semisweet. Cool on baking sheet until set; place decoratively on pie. Serve with whipped topping. ▼

Easy Substitute

For dark chocolate lovers, replace the milk chocolate chips with semisweet.

Terrific Topper

For an even more chocolaty flavor, dress up this creamy pie with chocolate whipped topping, then decorate with chocolate-covered nuts, chocolate shavings or sprinkles.

Nutty Idea

In place of pecans, use any of your favorite nuts: walnuts, hazelnuts, almonds, peanuts or, if you prefer, mixed nuts.

GOOD IDEA Serve this for dessert at a progressive dinner party, where guests take turns "hosting" parts of the meal in their homes.

Variations

For a Crowd

To satisfy chocolate-loving friends, make this recipe in a 13- x 9-inch pan and cut into small squares. Same great taste, but there is more to share!

Double Nut Taste

For a different look and taste, add toasted slivered almonds to the filling and top with toasted coconut. The flavors are crunchy and delicious.

Summer Strawberry Pie

You Will Need

❦❦❦❦❦

FOR THE CRUST

2   9-inch prepared frozen
    piecrusts, unbaked

FOR THE STRAWBERRY
PUREE AND PIE LAYERS

3   pints fresh strawberries,
    washed and hulled,
    divided

2   tablespoons strawberry
    liqueur or Kirsch
    (optional)

I   cup plus 2 tablespoons
    sugar, divided

⅛   teaspoon salt

2   tablespoons cold water

I   tablespoon unflavored
    gelatin

I   cup boiling water

I   cup whipping cream

3   cups sweetened whipped
    cream or frozen whipped
    topping, thawed

SPECIAL AIDS

parchment paper

9-inch pie plate

pie weights

strawberry-shaped cookie
    cutter

SERVES 10

**PREPARATION TIME
45 MINUTES plus chilling**

MAKING THE CRUST

1. Preheat oven to 350°F. Line a baking sheet with parchment paper. Fit 1 crust into a 9-inch pie plate; line crust with pie weights.

2. Roll remaining crust to a ¼-inch thickness; using a strawberry-shaped cookie cutter, cut 10 shapes from the crust. Arrange cutouts on the prepared baking sheet. ▼

3. Using a toothpick, mark "seeds" on cutouts. Place cutouts and crust in oven. Bake the cutouts until golden, 15-18 minutes. Remove cutouts from the oven; continue baking crust until golden, about 15 minutes longer. Remove pie weights; cool crust and cutouts completely.

PREPARING THE STRAWBERRY PUREE AND GELATIN LAYER

1. In a food processor fitted with a metal blade, puree 2 pints strawberries, liqueur, 2 tablespoons sugar and salt until smooth, about 30 seconds.

2. In a small bowl, pour cold water over gelatin; let stand until softened, about 5 minutes. Add boiling water and remaining sugar; stir to dissolve. Add ½ cup puree; mix well. ▼

3. Chill mixture until thickened but not set, about 1 hour. Transfer remaining puree to a glass measuring cup; chill. In a medium bowl, using an electric mixer set on medium speed, beat cream until thickened, about 2 minutes. Fold cream into gelatin mixture. Chop remaining berries; fold into cream mixture. Pour mixture into crust; chill at least 3 hours.

4. Spread whipped cream over filling. Drizzle half of remaining puree on top of pie in a zigzag pattern. ▼

5. Garnish pie with crust cutouts; serve remaining puree on the side.

Super Topper

Use the strawberry puree as an easy topping for sponge cake, bread pudding, crepes, waffles or pound cake.

Birthday Blast

Here's a neat idea for a birthday: Remove the hulls from fresh strawberries and insert a birthday candle in each. Stand the berries in a ring on top of the pie!

Saucy Idea

Use this strawberry puree for a simple shortcake. Drizzle it over biscuits and berries topped with whipped cream.

GOOD IDEA For ice-cream parlor flavor, top servings of this pie with hot fudge sauce and finely chopped nuts.

Variations

Fast Fridge Treat

For a dessert in a hurry, skip the crust and assemble the layers in a 9-inch square pan; chill as directed. Serve on a pool of the puree and top with sliced berries.

Pretty in Pink

Make your pie as light as a cloud. Fold $1/4$ cup of the puree into the whipped cream. Spread it over the filling layer; garnish with sliced strawberries.

index